Sourcing Smarts

Keeping it SIMPLE and SAFE with China Sourcing and Manufacturing

Edith G. Tolchin

with Don Debelak
and Eric Debelak

1

Sourcing Smarts: *Keeping it* SIMPLE *and* SAFE *with China Sourcing and Manufacturing.*

Printed in the United States of America.

www.sourcingsmarts.com

ISBN 978-0-615-36538-1

Cover Design by Josh Wallace, www.joshwallace.com

Table of Contents

Preface   5

Part 1 - Sourcing Wisely   6

Chapter 1 – To Source or Not to Source   6

Chapter 2 – Are You Ready?   17

Chapter 3 - Safe or Sorry - Critical   25
Information on the Consumer Product
Safety Improvement Act

Chapter 4 – How to Find a China Factory On   37
Your Own

Chapter 5 – Narrowing Down Your Choices   44
and Negotiating with the 'Winning' Factory

Chapter 6 – Placing a Purchase Order,   55
Payment and Shipping Terms

Chapter 7 – US Customs and Border   62
Protection Issues

Chapter 8 – Quality Issues, Safety and   68
Production Testing and Product Liability
Insurance

Chapter 9 – You're Ready to Ship... Now What?   74

Chapter 10 – China Sourcing Checklist   79

Chapter 11 – How to Protect Your Product Idea   83

Chapter 12 – Helpful Links   98

Part 2 - Marketing Wisely   100

Chapter 13 – Selling to Catalogs   102

Chapter 14 – Selling into the Gift Market   110

Chapter 15 – Distribute Your Product to Convenience Stores   129

Chapter 16 – Selling Your New Product through Carts and Kiosks   137

Chapter 17 – Selling Big: Finding the Right Marketing Partners   141

Chapter 18 – Landing an Inside Contact – the Easiest Way to Sell Your Product   152

About the Authors   159

Preface

I hope that this book provides comfort and knowledge for those inventors who are trying to make up their minds about manufacturing on their own, whether domestically or offshore. A lot of work is involved, but if done correctly and *SAFELY*, may you reap many rewards!

I will never forget you, Don Tolchin.

To my babies who aren't babies anymore Dori- you are a beautiful, refined, caring and classy young woman who will accomplish anything you set out to, and then some. Stay wise in all of your life choices. Max – Dr. Max Freeman – *ALWAYS* shoot for the stars and *NEVER* settle for mediocre. You will always be a leader; remember to send me a postcard!

Edie Tolchin

Chapter 1

To Source or Not to Source

You have a great invention. You've done lots of research, have a patent or patent-pending status and a working prototype. You have made several unsuccessful attempts at licensing, and have decided you might like to consider manufacturing on your own so you can have better control of sales and marketing.

Now, the big question …..

Should you source your product in China?

Many factors should be considered before sourcing in China. I will list the cons first, and then the pros.

Cons:

1. Difficult Communication: If you are not experienced in corresponding with China or Taiwan, your first attempt – typically by e-mail nowadays – may be very trying. Although the office personnel at most Asian factories do speak English, it is not the same "English" that we speak here in the USA. Many do not understand our local idioms or jargon, so remember to keep it simple and do not commit to anything you do not understand. Best-case scenario: Pay a little more

and hire a translator, or use an international trade consultant who specializes in working with Asian factories.

2. Quality and Accessibility Often Depend on the Type of Product: Many Asian factories produce excellent quality sewn and textile items. Their workers can be very talented and creative. However, forget about specialty fabrics or matching prints that you found in the USA. It can be done, but your costs will escalate

Cons:

1) Difficult Communication

2) Quality and Accessibility

3) Delivery Delays

4) Minimum Order Quantities

if you have custom-made fabric prints produced in China. You should also be aware that typically, the best grades of cotton are not found in China or Taiwan. But what about electronic inventions? Very high quality. Printing for packaging is not great, but has been improving over the years. The bottom line is – you really need to see counter-samples before committing to a purchase order. If your product must be specially made with a mold or tooling, first ask to see samples of similar stock items the factory has produced so you can be sure they can achieve the quality and workmanship you are looking for. Always arrange for production testing with an independent safety/testing lab (more info on this to follow in Chapter 2). Always ask for references ... and always check them!

Pros:

1) Improved Workmanship

2) Attitude - business relationship

3) New Jobs in USA

4) PRICING!

3. Delivery delays: There will be many delays – especially for first orders – from the time you submit your prototype and the factory sends you back a counter-sample. Be prepared to go "back and forth" by e-mail numerous times before quality control issues are ironed out. You might find, for example, that a button is on the wrong side, a light bulb must be larger, printing needs to be darker, or the outer box has to be thicker. It's also important to know that during their holidays many Asian factories may close for two weeks or more (as with

the Chinese New Year festival), which could delay your shipment. Ask if they can provide you with their holiday schedule so you are aware well in advance of their down times. Also, during typhoon/monsoon seasons everyone is on watch for delays. If you are told that your delivery will be 30-45 days, figure more like 60-75 days, allowing for holidays, coordinating pre-production and mass-production samples, independent testing, etc.

4. MOQs (Minimum Order Quantities): You might have heard that sourcing in Asia requires you to purchase huge quantities, and this can be difficult if you are just starting out and merely want to "test the waters" with your product. For many industries the quantity rule holds true. For most new products, the factory itself must source the components for your new invention from several different factories that in turn issue an MOQ to your factory for their products. So, that is why sometimes you must purchase large quantities (50,000 vs. 5,000 pieces). In the textiles industry this can frequently happen. With each new invention that is sourced, in order to make a counter-sample and provide you with a price quote, the factory must get quotes on components such as zippers, buttons, ribbons, thread, fabric, packaging, and labels. Each of your factory's suppliers has an already-

established MOQ. So, as you can see, it is not easy for the factory to just submit to you a quote for a new product within a day or two.

Pros:

1. Quality: Over the many years I have been involved in sourcing, Asian factories have improved their workmanship. Just make sure that your correspondence is completely clear and that you have good working prototypes with easy-to-understand specifications. The old saying goes, "less is more," but in this case that most definitely does NOT apply. Never worry that you are sending TOO MUCH information. The more accurate data you can furnish to the prospective supplier in Asia, the better the quality of your product will be.

2. Attitude: Most Asian suppliers are very interested in establishing a good business relationship with you. They will be eager to please you with the hope that you will continue to work with them for reorders once your product has become successful!

3. New jobs? Many worry that if they source their inventions in Asia, it will take away from jobs in the USA. This is not necessarily true. Sourcing and manufacturing products in Asia in turn opens up numerous business opportunities here at home

in logistics, distribution, computer graphics, sales and marketing. For example, dockworkers will need to unload your shipment off the vessel and send it by truck or rail to your warehouse, storage facility or distribution center. Your graphic artist will design your logo, labeling and packaging. You will need to engage a Consumer Product Safety Commission's accredited safety lab for your product design evaluation. And don't forget about the U.S. marketing firm that could get you some good PR. Once your product(s) are selling, reliable domestic trucking firms can make deliveries to retail outlets all over the USA!

4. PRICING, PRICING, PRICING! Did I say, "pricing?" Many new products can be sourced in China, depending on the industry, for anywhere from 1/2 to 1/8 of what it would cost to be manufactured in the USA. This is an obvious advantage to new business start-ups!

For many, the thought of manufacturing overseas is daunting, but with the proper guidance and reliable contacts it can be an option you may want to consider. As with any business plan, there are pros and cons that must be weighed. Remember, asking the right questions and understanding the answers is essential to success in any endeavor. Make sure the lines of communication are clear and you could find the cost savings of manufacturing overseas gives you enough breathing room to launch a successful product and grow a profitable business.

Inventor Story:

Should I Outsource?

Joe Yao, MD is an orthopedic surgeon who himself suffers from hand pain and numbness while driving a car or working on the computer. From his medical practice, Yao knew that he was not alone with this pain.

Several years ago, Yao's hands went numb while driving on the Interstate and he decided that he needed to come up with a solution. Numbness is caused by vibrations on the major hand nerves and most driving gloves have pads placed over these nerves, which transfer the vibration directly to the nerves. Yao thought that he could place pads around these nerves so that the vibration would be diverted away from the nerves, thereby reducing or eliminating numbness.

Yao did his market research, created a prototype and found that his product would need to sell for $17.50 to be competitive.

When he started contacting glove manufacturers in the U.S., most were simply not interested. Of all the manufacturers he contacted, only two seemed interested. After receiving the schematics and a video explaining construction of the glove, the manufacturers were still hesitant to offer a quote. Yao kept on prodding the manufacturers to give him a quote. Finally one responded; $32 without shipping. For a product that retails at $17.50, that is clearly a non-starter. Manufacturing costs need to be 20-25% of the retail price.

When he started contacting glove manufacturers in the U.S., most were simply not interested.

At this point Yao realized that he would need to outsource manufacturing. He started by contacting international trade consultant, Edith Tolchin, of EGT Global Trading, and together they started corresponding with Chinese manufacturers for quotes. While Yao could only find two U.S. manufacturers even interested in looking at his product and only one who was willing to give a quote, he found the Chinese manufacturers had a much better attitude about gaining new business. Not all of the manufacturers responded, and some responded with very limited English, but the others responded promptly in reasonable English.

> **Yao found the Chinese manufacturers had a much better attitude about gaining new business.**

Yao's current manufacturer is very eager to help and do the job correctly. They do their best to work out any problems promptly with Yao and stand behind their product 100%. Their attitude shows they are thankful for the business and are doing their best not to lose it — the ideal attitude for your business associates to have.

Of course, outsourcing manufacturing hasn't been all easy for Yao. His product, Qwi™ Nerve Protection Gloves, http://www.qwinerveprotector.com/, is primarily sold to motorcyclists and truck drivers who tend to be very patriotic. Some potential customers refuse to buy the product simply because it is manufactured overseas. Sometimes explaining that U.S. manufacturers were unwilling to produce the product helps, but not always.

Yao also has had to be patient as he makes product changes. Originally he thought

> **A misjudgment in sales projections can cause a shortage of one product and a surplus of another.**

that truck drivers would be the best market, but he soon found out that it was a hard market to crack and he had to switch gears to focus on motorcyclists. This required a change in the product, which would have taken one or two days if manufacturing were based in the U.S., but it took months working with an overseas manufacturer.

A constant challenge is projecting sales because it takes so long to receive a product shipment. Yao needs to order at least three months in advance so he doesn't run out of inventory, but a misjudgment can cause a shortage of one product and a surplus of another.

> A required product change, which would have taken one or two days in manufacturing were based in the U.S., took months while working with an overseas manufacturer.

Yao has also had a string of quality issues, which actually forced him to change manufacturers. Even the new manufacturer has had problems with dye transferring from the gloves to the wearer's skin.

> Yao's business is still in the early stages and success is by no means guaranteed, but he would have never gotten this far without outsourcing.

Despite these drawbacks, Yao has been happy with his choice of manufacturing overseas. His business is still in the early stages and success is by no means guaranteed, but he would never have gotten this far without outsourcing. Now Yao is honing his sales strategy and gaining a growing number of very satisfied customers who love the product so much that they tell all their friends about it.

Chapter 2

Are you ready?

You have worked long hours on developing your idea! Attorneys, prototypes, attempts at licensing, and it seems as though you are still just beginning! How do you finally get your product "out there?" A guest speaker at your monthly inventors' group meeting suggests that you might want to attempt a small production run, on your own, in China. Now what???

This chapter will address some issues you should NOT overlook when sourcing and producing your invention in China.

Product Design Evaluation with a CPSC-accredited independent testing/safety lab: Yes, you believe your product is safe, but does it conform to the various regulations for imported products? There are so many US government agencies that oversee imported products, and each of those agencies has its own rules to follow; doing this research on your own can cause a whirlwind in your brain! You've got the Federal Trade Commission (www.ftc.gov), the Consumer Product Safety Commission (www.cpsc.gov), US Customs and Border Protection (www.cbp.gov) and many more. How do you make sure your invention meets these various standards? The CPSC has a list of accredited testing/safety labs listed on their website. Contact several (there are many) and ask if they specialize in evaluations of new inventions. If so, then describe your invention to them (i.e., electronic, plastics, textiles, toy, etc.), and ask them for a price quote on having a Product Design Evaluation done.

"Why," you ask, do you need to work with an independent testing/safety lab? "My invention is perfectly safe!" It sure looks like that to the average consumer. But these labs are trained to look for issues that you or I would never ever think about. Use the example of a new type of children's plastic craft scissors, with rounded (safety) tips, etc. Seems safe enough right? Not to the safety/testing labs! What type of plastic is used? Are there any hazardous, environmentally unfriendly chemicals used in the components? Are there any parts that can come loose and pose a choking hazard? Has it been "age-graded" so that (for example) if you intend for it to be used by children ages 3 and older, what happens if 15 month-old little sister Susie grabs hold of them and bites off the handle!?!?!?! Has it been properly marked to show country of origin (as required by US Customs and Border Protection's regulations)? The list goes on and on.

A Design Evaluation is my favorite tool for beginning the product development of your invention. The labs will thoroughly review your product for any "red flags" or possible safety issues and provide a list of recommended modifications to get your product into compliance. They will evaluate for the Consumer Product Safety Improvement Act and its regulations. They will also address the numerous labeling, packaging and other government regulations for imported merchandise, all to be outlined in your report. The last part of the evaluation will be a thorough list of recommended production testing that should be done in one of their satellite offices in China, once your order has been placed with the China supplier. Although the headquarters for most of these labs may be located in the USA, most labs have satellite offices in many cities throughout China, which will frequently be very close to the factory where your order is being produced. It is advantageous to have the tests done in the China affiliate offices rather than at the US headquarters because the costs for production testing are frequently less expensive in China than in the lab's USA offices. There is also less transit time and shipping expenses involved in sending the samples for testing to another office within China rather than back to the USA.

With report in hand, you now know the modifications which must be done to your prototype, and are armed with production testing information to bring your invention into compliance with the various US government agencies' seemingly infinite requirements. This also helps with Product Liability Insurance, which every new business selling consumer products should have. And, your goal with proper production testing and addressing all safety issues is to make sure your new product NEVER appears on the

Consumer Product Safety Commission's Product Recall List! (go to: cpsc.gov/cpscpub/prerel/prerel.html). A Product Recall can make or break any new business! IMPORTANT: PRODUCT SAFETY IS NOW A LAW! Please see Chapter 3 for a complete overview of product safety and the Consumer Product Safety Improvement Act.

Before you start the sourcing process, safety evaluations and testing, make sure your product is right for your intended market. If you rush into manufacturing your product only to find out that the market is looking for a different product (much like Joe Yao did, as mentioned in Chapter 1), you may need to make substantial changes to your product's design.

Changes may raise new safety issues, forcing your product to be re-evaluated by a CPSC-accredited safety lab. You will save time and money if you get it right the first time, so do your market research in advance.

If you are having a hard time discerning what your intended market wants, consider professional help. The One Stop Invention Shop does low cost product evaluations that help you understand your target market and how to develop your product to meet that market's needs. These evaluations also address many other factors that impact your chances for success, like distribution.

"Perfected" prototype: You have heard that all you need to begin the sourcing process are detailed drawings or sketches of your product? Sometimes yes, but frequently NO! It is always better to have a *perfect* prototype to send to China. You have obtained your Design Evaluation from the safety/testing lab, so why on earth, after doing the ground work, would you send just the drawings? If you do, you will spend much time and energy on back-and-forth e-mails, attempting to convey the intricate details of your product, which unfortunately a sketch just cannot address. With China sourcing, what you see is what you get. So, even if you send over a rough prototype, it will take you many long e-mails trying to explain the modifications you want done, before placing an order. You will frequently encounter communication difficulties, as mentioned before. Yes, you most certainly can hire a translator to list all of the modifications in Chinese. This is what I would consider a good back-up plan, though it can be expensive. But the easiest, quickest and most efficient method for a pleasant sourcing experience is to have a perfect prototype done in the USA. There are many capable prototype specialists in all commodities, and many can be found at the website for the United Inventors Association (www.uiausa.org). USA prototype costs may be expensive, but will save you money in the long run, thus avoiding the costly FedEx charges for numerous back-and-forth submissions to and from China until they get it right, not to mention possible

22

delays in launching your product, before your prototype is exactly as you want it.

Inventor Story:

Can my product be produced in China?

Karen Nadler-Sachs was feeding her two and a half year-old breakfast early one morning. To protect the upholstered dining room chair her daughter was sitting on, Nadler-Sachs placed a towel on the seat of the chair. After some squirming, the towel no longer completely covered the chair and a gob of jam fell directly on the exposed upholstery. At that time, Nadler-Sachs decided to invent something to protect her chairs and save her the trouble of constantly cleaning them.

Nadler-Sachs started sewing dozens of prototypes out of a variety of materials to try to get her design right. Once she had a good prototype, she took it everywhere with her – to her friends' houses, to furniture stores – to make sure it would fit on all types of chairs. Then she worked with prototypers and design engineers to perfect the final design.

At this point, Nadler-Sachs started investigating manufacturing. She quickly realized that U.S. manufacturers were not able to produce her product at a price that would make it competitive and allow her to make a profit. She set her sights overseas, but she had a big problem: she only wanted to make a small production run to test the waters.

Nadler-Sachs decided that she needed some help and contacted international trade consultant Edith Tolchin. Tolchin knew a few manufacturers that would handle low volume production and set up production at one of those plants.

Nadler-Sachs submitted them a perfect prototype, which she spent lots of time working out with her prototypers, design engineers and even with the advice of a few friends. She knew what goes in comes out, so a stitch in the wrong place will be replicated on every single product.

Once the samples came back, Nadler-Sachs poured over every seam and every letter of the label to make sure it was all perfect. Then she ordered her first 1,000 units of product, which is named, "Save the Chairs!" http://www.savethechairs.com.

Although Nadler-Sachs only wanted 1,000 units, she was able to manufacture in China to give her product a test run in the U.S. She did her homework and made sure her prototype was perfect so that her end product was perfect.

Chapter 3

SAFE OR SORRY?

ALL NEW, Critical Information on the Consumer Product
Safety Improvement Act

For years, inventors choosing to manufacture on their own have gotten by on a wing and a prayer concerning product safety issues. Those who were diligent did their own research, perhaps by surfing the Consumer Product Safety Commission's (CPSC) website for product guidelines, or hoping that they could trust the factory to do the right thing, or by hiring a consultant, but they were still left with the fear that their newly-manufactured products could be recalled at any time.

The Consumer Product Safety Improvement Act (CPSIA) was created in 2008 to address the rash of product recalls due to, for example, lead levels and other toxic chemicals found in children's products, small parts and choking hazards, and defective equipment such as baby cribs, car seats and other baby carriers. It is an ever-evolving, very complex law, and the CPSC continues to issue very frequent amendments, with which you must keep current.

Those inventors who felt that they had safe products – perhaps those that held focus groups for product trials,

25

or asked other parents to try their prototypes – now became faced with the harsh reality that ALL CHILDREN'S PRODUCTS, *and many other consumer products*, will now require production testing.

From the production testing, the tracking labels (for children's products) and General Conformity Certificates (GCC – or sometimes called a "Certificate of Compliance") are created. These documents and labels are part of the CPSIA requirements and are used to track the manufacturer of the product, in case of recalls or other safety issues. The General Conformity Certificate must be made available for Customs and Border Protection if they decide to ask for it, when the product is imported, and it must be available to present to retail and distribution channels, whether your product is imported or domestic, when requested. And, tracking labels become a part of your product (attached permanently), as well as the packaging.

This chapter will address frequently asked questions, offer guidelines on how to manufacture a safe product, and how to conform to the various regulations of the CPSIA. You will find it to be written in the simplest terms possible, to get to the bottom line of what you need...*A SAFELY MANUFACTURED PRODUCT.*

Now before we begin, please understand that the most efficient step you can take to ensure product safety is to follow the Consumer Product Safety Commission's website for CPSIA updates. Please go to:

http://www.cpsc.gov/about/cpsia/cpsia.html
FREQUENTLY - as often as weekly if possible, and subscribe to their updates.

1) ***I have a children's product (or other consumer product) and need to know: where do I begin with all of this?***

The very first thing that I consider essential is a Product Design Evaluation (DE) with a Consumer Product Safety Commission's accredited laboratory that can provide this service. (Not all accredited labs can provide this service.) Your prototype is presented to the lab, along with any written product information, brochures, component lists, alternate materials list, and sample packaging mock-ups if available.

A DE will address all CPSIA safety issues, will provide any red flags or safety issues and will make recommendations for fixing any problems. It will also cover special regulations issued by other government agencies such as Customs and Border Protection (www.cbp.gov), the Federal Trade Commission (www.ftc.gov), and the Food and Drug Administration (www.fda.gov), among others, which may affect your product. Labeling and marking will also be included. You will also be given a list of both mandatory and optional production tests, such as lead levels, flammability, phthalates, and choking hazards, some of which will be required so that your product complies with the CPSIA.

Fees, at press time, for a DE can run in the $1000 - $1500 range, on average, and should be individually quoted by the lab. The lab will provide you with an application form, which you can complete to include your personal and company information, product information and there will be a space where you can specify exactly what you want the lab to do for you. In that space provided, you must definitely ask the lab to quote you the cost of the DE beforehand, and make sure you include a request for a "CPSIA evaluation" as part of the application form.

Typically within 2-3 weeks, you will have the report, and are usually given a chance to ask questions about the report for a brief period of time thereafter.

2) *Can I choose a lab for production testing of my product?*

Yes and no. First, the lab MUST be CPSC-accredited. For a complete list of Accredited Testing Labs, please go to: http://www.cpsc.gov/cgi-bin/labapplist.aspx. From that very thorough list, you can select a lab to handle your DE. If the lab is not CPSC-accredited, it will be a waste of time.

3) *My product is NOT for children. How do I know if the CPSIA applies to my product, and will I still require production testing?*

First, check the CPSC's list of "Regulated Products," at http://www.cpsc.gov/BUSINFO/reg.html.

If your product is a new invention, start with that list, and if you see your product, or a similar product on that list, that is clear indication that you will require production testing, and that it must comply with the CPSIA regulations.

If your product is not on the "Regulated Products" list, you can go to another link that is specifically for products with special rules, standards and/or bans:

http://www.cpsc.gov/cpscpub/prerel/prhtml10/10083.html.

If you are still in doubt, you may contact the CPSC directly in Bethesda, MD, at info@cpsc.gov.

According to the Consumer Product Safety Commission's website, "A General Conformity Certificate will be required for some non-children's products." It continues, "these products include: architectural glazing materials, ATVs, adult bunk beds, candles with metal wicks, CB antennas, contact adhesives, cigarette lighters, multi-purpose lighters, matchbooks, garage door openers, portable gas containers, lawn mowers, mattresses, unstable refuse bins, refrigerator door latches, swimming pool slides, products subject to regulations under the Poison Prevention Packaging Act

(PPPA), paint and household furniture subject to lead paint regulations."

When in doubt, the $1000 - $1500 you spend for a Product Design Evaluation (as indicated under #1 above) is the best investment you can make for developing your new product. Even if your product is NOT affected by CPSIA regulations, your DE document will be your proof.

4) **How do I prepare a General Conformity Certificate?**

The best way is to go to this link: http://www.cpsc.gov/ABOUT/Cpsia/faq/102faq.html.

5) **Who issues the General Conformity Certificate?**

According to the CPSC, "for products manufactured overseas, the certificate must be issued by the importer. For products produced inside the United States, the certificate must be issued by the U.S. manufacturer. Neither a foreign manufacturer nor a private labeler is required to issue a certificate. Neither need be identified on the certificate issued by the importer or domestic manufacturer."

6) *What data is required on the GCC?*

In English (as well in any OTHER language you choose), you must include your business information (for example, your letterhead), the tests or regulations that pertain to your product (such as flammability, lead content, choking hazards, etc.), the CPSC-accredited laboratory (called "third-party conformity assessment body" by the CPSC) who performed the production tests, the lab's address and full contact information including address, phone, as well as name of person (at your company) who maintains test results records.

7) *What about "tracking labels"* (for children's products only)?

First, make sure to go to: http://www.cpsc.gov/ABOUT/Cpsia/faq/103faq.html. This is a list of FAQs for preparation of tracking labels for your product. Tracking labels are for children's products intended primarily for those aged 12 years and under, and must be permanently affixed to your product. The tracking label must be printed on your packaging as well.

8) *What information must be included on the tracking labels?*

Name and address of manufacturer, importer or private labeler, date of manufacture (i.e. month, year), batch number (such as purchase order or production run number), country of manufacture (such as "Made in China"), city, province and country, then *your* contact information (such as website, e-mail address, phone/fax numbers, etc.)

9) *Do I still need to comply with the CPSIA if my product is manufactured in the USA – or does it only pertain to imported products?*

The CPSIA pertains to products *REGARDLESS OF WHERE* they are made – whether they are domestically produced or imported from overseas.

10) *Do I need to get EVERY production run tested?*

Yes and no. If you can certify that the manufacturer is using the EXACT same components (raw materials, fabrics, etc.) for every production run, then you do not have to test every batch. However this is very difficult to prove. For example, if you are working with an overseas factory, the odds are that it works with different suppliers for your order, and each of these suppliers (for even just your one order) may use a different batch of components, so it's best to test each production run to insure conformity (and to make sure it passes the safety tests to qualify it for certification).

Again, I cannot emphasize enough the importance of following the CPSIA's regulations to the letter. As of this writing, the CPSIA is still evolving, and the Consumer

Product Safety Commission often sponsors very useful online webinars. Understand that what regulations may pertain today, may not be valid (or may be modified) tomorrow or next week. As referenced above, put this link in your "Favorites" file and check often: http://www.cpsc.gov/about/cpsia/cpsia.html.

Subscribe to their e-mail alerts concerning the CPSIA as well.

If even after reading this chapter you still feel uneasy and have additional questions – please feel free to contact me, Edie Tolchin, at EGT@warwick.net. I can assist you with a Product Design Evaluation from a CPSC-accredited safety lab, with arrangements for production testing, and the creation of both the General Conformity Certificate and Tracking Labels for your product. I would also be happy to send you a list of the web links mentioned in this chapter, many of which are included on my website, www.egtglobaltrading.com. Document samples follow.

Bottom line: the more you know, the better off you'll be; it's *always* better to be safe than sorry!

Smith Baby Umbrella Co.

229 East Chatham Road

Sunny, PA 18600

Phone 814-555-2298 / Fax 814-555-2299

www.smithbabyumbrellaco.com

GENERAL CONFORMITY CERTIFICATE –
(SAMPLE)

Product Style number: UMB-001 Baby-smith™

Product Description: Baby-smith™ is a wind-resistant nylon miniature umbrella which attaches to baby's stroller and guards baby from sun, wind and rain.

We, Smith Baby Umbrella Co. declare that the above designated product is in conformity with the following CPSC / CPSIA product safety regulations:

(insert regulations / tests here below)-

1. FLAMMABILITY (16 CFR SECTION 1500.3(c)6)(vi))

2. TOTAL LEAD CONTENT IN SURFACE COATING BY COMPOSITE TESTING ("Ban of Lead-containing paint and certain consumer products bearing Lead-containing paint", Consumer Product Safety Improvement Act (CPSIA) of 2008)

3. SOLUBLE HEAVY METALS CONTENT (ASTM F963-08, Section 4.3.5.2)

Date of manufacture (month/year): (month / year)

Place of manufacture (state/country): NANTONG CITY, JIANGSU, CHINA 440257

Date of testing (month/year): (month / year)

Test Lab: (lab name, address, city, province, country, zip, phone/fax numbers, contact person, website)

Test Report # 888-42944

Person maintaining test records: Henry Smith, 229 East Chatham Road, Sunny, PA 18600. E-mail: h.smith@smithbabyumbrellaco.com, website: www.smithbabyumbrellaco.com

Date of Issue: (month, date, year)

CPSIA TRACKING LABEL

Imported by:

Smith Baby Umbrella Co.
229 East Chatham Road
Sunny, PA 18600
Phone 814-555-2298
Fax 814-555-2299
www.smithbabyumbrellaco.com

Manufactured on:

(Insert month / year)

Batch number: PO# SBU-077

MADE IN CHINA

(City, Province, Country, Postal Code)

Contact info:

sales@smithbabyumbrellaco.com

(SAMPLE)

Chapter 4

How to Find a China Factory on Your Own

Finding a good, reliable Chinese manufacturer can be intimidating for a first time inventor. Listed below is everything you need to know to find a good manufacturer, but many inventors still look for help to import their first product. An international trade consultant will know all of the ins and outs of locating and working with an overseas manufacturer.

Creating a List of Potential Manufacturers: To find a good manufacturer, go to one or all of the websites listed on the right.

Start by entering the type of product you want manufactured and the country from where you want to purchase it. This can difficult for new inventions if they create a new product category, since the existing search options will not help you. So, you should find a general category that your invention may fit

alibaba.com
chinasources.com –
(globalsources.com)
ttnet.net
tradeeasy.com
made-in-china.com

into – for example, hats, radios, toys, tablecloths, brooms, and so on. That should help you locate manufacturers of products similar to your invention.

Another way to develop a list of potential manufacturers is to network with other inventors who have inventions similar to yours. If they have manufactured overseas, ask about their experience with their manufacturer.

Making Initial Contact: After you have created a good list of potential manufacturers, contact them and ask for references of American firms with whom they have worked with. If they are concerned with confidentiality, ask for some brand names they manufacture, that you might recognize in US stores.

When they respond, assess their ease in communication, their mastery of the English language, and their promptness in replying. If they take a week to reply to an initial e-mail, that will usually be an indication that they will not be very good at getting back to you, and this could delay the development of your product.

Many Asian suppliers will claim (sometimes for their convenience – they can't be bothered, they're too busy) that they do not want to violate confidentiality. But if they are working with big USA companies (Walmart, Home Depot, etc.), then you most definitely want to know this! This is a good thing. A sign of a capable, confident source is if they volunteer the names of recognizable USA companies they have manufactured for. Besides, just by giving a business partner's name, it does not reveal any product details.

If they do not want to give you the names of USA buyers, then be persistent and ask them for some USA brand names (i.e., Disney, Liz Claiborne, America's Pride) of products that you might recognize in retail shops. This obviously does not create a confidentiality issue because the products are already out there! If they cannot give you either references and/or USA brand names, don't waste your time dealing with them. Go with someone who has a proven track record.

Upon receiving a list of references, contact them and ask how their experience was with the manufacturer. If other companies have had bad experiences, chances are you will too.

Asking for Quotes: After contacting the references that the manufacturers have provided, hopefully you will have narrowed down your list to at least five good prospects. Put together a package to send to each of those manufacturers that includes samples of your prototype, along with all product literature, specifications, measurements, components, etc. Many sources can work with drawings, but it is more efficient to use actual prototypes, as mentioned in Chapter 2. Also include any safety issues you will want addressed, taken from your Design Evaluation report from the independent testing / safety lab, and any production tests that they must comply with, also from the Design

Evaluation. Have vital information translated into Chinese.

Make sure to include an introduction letter, indicating the quantity you are looking to buy, the ports into which you would like to ship your order, and any special features of your product that need to be included, which might not be obvious to the supplier when they first look at your prototype.

Give as much info as possible – communication can be difficult and the more information you give the more likely your product will turn out right.

Finding an International Trade Consultant: If at this point you are feeling overwhelmed, you may want to hire an international trade consultant. To find one, read the classified ads in Inventors' Digest magazine, whether via hard copy or online at www.inventorsdigest.com. Look under their Classifieds. You can also contact the United Inventors Association: www.uiausa.org, or look under "Inventor-Friendly Companies" or "Find A Certified Pro" at the website.

There are also a few important trade organizations to consider: First, the Federation of International Trade Associations (www.fita.org) is a good place to start. And, you may contact the National Customs Brokers & Forwarders Association of America, Inc. at: www.ncbfaa.org. Although you may not need a Customs Broker or Freight Forwarder immediately, many customs brokerage firms employ international trade consultants or may be able to recommend one.

Last, if your invention Is a textile or sewn item, bag, baby accessory, arts & crafts product, small household invention or fashion item, you may contact me, Edie Tolchin, at EGT@warwick.net.

Inventor Story:

Finding a Manufacturer

Brian Donnelly was an industrial design professor at San Francisco State University when he started designing his LifeSpan Furnishing product line. His first product was the Easy Up chair, a chair with longer arm rests and legs pointed outward to make it easy to get up out of the chair, but hard to knock it over in the process. The Easy Up had already won many awards for its senior-friendly design and he was ready to go into full production.

Donnelly started contacting U.S. manufacturers, trying to strike a licensing deal, but they all wanted too much money. He started to peruse furniture stores that would make something similar to his original design, which was made of metal. He found some products made by a Chinese manufacturer that were similar to what he envisioned for his product and learned that they were distributed by Iem, a company based out of California.

When Donnelly contacted Iem, they not only were willing to help him set up production, they wanted to invest in the product. Iem used its network to get the Easy Up chair into production. When Donnelly decided to expand his line to include wooden products, something that Iem and its network didn't do, Iem was able to use its contacts to find a reliable wood furniture manufacturer for Donnelly.

Since Donnelly started his business, he has found another way to locate manufacturers: industry trade shows. At all the international furniture fairs he attends, there are booths from Asian country trade councils looking for U.S. companies to manufacture their products in their home countries. These councils are willing to go the extra mile in getting you set up in their country, although you still need to be careful in taking the proper steps to determine if the factories themselves are reliable.

Inventor Story:

Finding a Representative

In 2003, Keith Wickenhauser owned a bar and grill. He noticed that people were constantly losing their keys, cell phones, cigarettes, and lighters – but no one ever lost their drink.

Wickenhauser thought that a product that could keep a drink and some small personal items together would be a great idea. Over the years, he had sold can coolers and given them away as promotions and he knew that the market was strong for such products, so he decided to take his idea and turn it into a promotional can cooler, the Wickooler, http://wickooler.com/.

After finishing developing the product, Wickenhauser had a U.S. manufacturer make some prototypes. He showed these to customers at convenience stores and had them rate the value of the product compared to other similar products. By doing this, he determined that $4.99 was the price that people would pay for his product.

After researching manufacturing costs in the U.S., Wickenhauser realized that he would need to take his product overseas to be manufactured. He did not feel comfortable is navigating the whole system himself, so he asked a friend who has experience in importing. His friend recommended a representative located in Asia that he had worked with in the past.

Wickenhauser has used this representative to locate a manufacturer, negotiate the price, oversee production schedules and handle quality control.

Chapter 5

Narrowing Down Your Choices and Negotiating with the 'Winning' Factory

After you have sent your five prototype samples and information to different factories, you should start receiving quotes in 2-4 weeks. The quotes may be similar or quite varied, but you don't want to choose a factory solely on price. There are issues of quality, promptness and reliability that can make or break your product and these issues simply cannot be overlooked. Below are some important questions to ask your potential manufacturers.

- Can you provide recommendations of proposed alternate materials?
- Can you please give me a list of holidays when your factory will be closed for the current year?
- What is your delivery lead time?

- What policies do you have in place for replacement of defective merchandise?
- Do you work with a China freight forwarder who could arrange our shipment?
- What are your MOQs (minimum order quantities)?
- Are you willing to cooperate with the Asian affiliate of our appointed independent safety / testing lab?
- Do you work with a translator?

1. **Can you provide recommendations of proposed alternate materials?**

For example, your prototype is made of leather, but you are seeking a less expensive, but attractive alternative. Will they offer you samples of other fabrics (canvas, nylon, polyester)? This will help determine their eagerness to please and their problem-solving skills, which are very important with a foreign supplier.

2. **Can you please give me a list of holidays when your factory will be closed for the current year?** This is very important, because China factories have many holidays where they are closed and therefore your production (and other product development stages) comes to a halt for as many as two to three weeks, especially during Chinese New Year, typically at the end of January / early February. This way, you can adjust your schedules accordingly.

3. **What is your delivery lead time?** In other words, from the time we approve both the pre-production and mass-production samples, how much longer will your factory require before my order is placed on a vessel (or air cargo)?

4. **What policies do you have in place for replacement of defective merchandise?** I normally write a stipulation in all my purchase orders that clearly spells out how the supplier will replace any defective items, beyond the typical industry standard, indicating that they (the seller) will be responsible for not only replacing the defective product, but also for arranging for the

collection, and return shipment of those items as well.

5. **Do you work with a China freight forwarder who could arrange our shipment?** For many small initial orders, it can be easier and more economical for the supplier to arrange for the ocean freight and marine insurance to be prepaid, and coordinated by their appointed freight forwarder at the port in China. Also, sometimes the factories get cheaper freight rates than if arranged in the USA. Your unit cost will increase by a few cents, but it will be worth not having to deal with steamship companies for quotes, making the arrangements with not-so-reliable trucking firms in China, inferior roads and transportation systems within China, and so on.

6. **What are your MOQs (minimum order quantities)?** This one is a biggie! If you are only in the position, as most start-ups are, to purchase a small number of pieces to begin with, you must state this up-front. Many Asian firms – especially the larger ones – will assume you are interested in purchasing their "typical" MOQs from the start. These "typical" MOQs can be upwards of 50,000 – 100,000 units! So, if you only want to buy 1,000 to "test the (market) waters," that should be the very first subject you discuss. You don't want to get too far along with prototypes, counter-samples, and so on, only to lead the

source on, thinking you will buy these huge quantities, and then he/she will quote you a price break, for 50,000 – 100,000 – 250,000 units! You can certainly volunteer that you will only be buying a small quantity to begin with, but if your product sells well, you will be back to them in the future for a quote for larger quantities.

7. **Are you willing to cooperate with the Asian affiliate of our appointed independent safety / testing lab?** The answer for this one should be obvious: if they say no, or are non-committal, run for the hills. If your invention is a children's product, a consumer product, or appears on the Consumer Product Safety Commission's list of Regulated products, it is an item with possible safety issues (for product liability insurance purposes), you will NEED to have production testing done. Your mission is to make sure your new product never appears on the Consumer Product Safety Commission's (www.cpsc.gov) Recall List. You can literally "lose you shirt" if this happens. Also, penalties for non-compliance with the Consumer Product Safety Improvement Act can run in the thousands of dollars.

8. **Do you work with a translator?** You can almost always expect a small communication problem, which is why I recommend working with an international trade consultant or another

inventor who has imported from China before, because "Chinese-English" terms are frequently very different from "American-English" terms. Your supplier's command of the English language should be a very strong factor in your ease of building a business relationship. But if you find you are having too much difficulty, you can ask your prospective supplier to find a translator – or better yet, have the documents and/or specifications translated into Chinese BEFORE you send them. It may cost a couple hundred dollars, but it will save time and money in the long run. Many universities in large cities have Chinese departments with professors fluent in Chinese. Contact a few and ask if they provide translations for a fee.

At this point, you may have found that none of your potential manufacturers will work out. Don't worry, just put together another list of manufacturers and start again. There are thousands of factories in China so you still have plenty of options left. If you still have at least one potential manufacturer left, you need to make your final choice and start the negotiating process.

Your Chinese manufacturer will almost always expect you to negotiate on the final price of the product and shipping terms. Depending on your background and where you are from in the U.S., this may not be easy for you and you may want to enlist the help of someone who has some negotiating experience.

You can start the price negotiation process by simply sending a counter-bid. Keep it realistic, since if you really are interested in the prospective supplier, you do not want to be insulting.

Another way to open negotiations is to suggest your desired price in your introduction letter when you submit your prototypes. For example, you might write: "I am expecting to pay for 5,000 pieces. at US$2.50 per piece", which should normally be a few cents lower than what you'd expect to pay. This way, if the supplier counters with a bid of US$2.60 per piece, it may still be within your acceptable price range.

Most China factories quote payment / shipping terms either as "FOB China" pricing, which WILL NOT include ocean freight and marine insurance, or "CIF USA" port pricing, which WILL include freight and insurance. This is also negotiable. I typically prefer "CIF USA" port pricing because the supplier makes all the arrangements, frequently via its freight forwarder and steamship company in China, and issues a marine insurance policy as well. All you will have to do, when the shipment arrives in the USA, is have your (USA) customs broker clear your shipment for you, prepay import duties, and arrange transportation from the port to your inland delivery destination.

With "FOB China" pricing, however, you and/or your freight forwarder would have to make all arrangements to book space with a steamship company in China, obtain marine insurance, etc., all of which can be a bit more costly if arranged from the USA instead of in China. Your supplier would then just be responsible for shipping the cargo to the appointed vessel at the Chinese port, and the rest is your responsibility. There will be more on this in Chapter 6.

Also be aware of the payment terms. Typical payment terms are 30% down payment at time the purchase order is signed, sent via wire transfer from your bank to the China supplier's bank in China. The factory then goes into production, and all steps are taken as mentioned in Chapter 2, including pre-production sampling, production testing, quality control, mass-production samples, etc. When you, the buyer, approve the final mass-production samples, the supplier prepares the shipping documentation, which should be reviewed by either your international trade consultant or your customs broker, and arranges space on a vessel (or air cargo). The supplier will present you with proof of shipment and at that point you can arrange for the balance of 70% to be transferred from your bank to theirs.

With large volume orders, payment via Letter of Credit (L/C) can be used, but that is for merchandise worth (typically) hundreds of thousands of dollars. Letters of Credit can carry very steep bank fees for discrepancies in documentation, so that is why they are typically used only for larger purchase orders. There is almost always a discrepancy between L/C terms and shipping documents, which have to match up perfectly. Even so much as a misspelled word can cause an L/C discrepancy. As a first time importer, you definitely want to use bank wire transfers.

Inventor Story:

I Need a Good Manufacturer!

Many women match every outfit they wear with a handbag, but often they either don't have a coordinated wallet or they don't have time to move all of their cards, pictures and other things to their coordinated wallet. This frustrated Shannon Greenfield every time it happened to her. She remembers saying: "Someone should make a wallet that allows us to easily change the outer appearance of our wallet without removing the contents." And Shannon became that someone!

Greenfield made a variety of prototypes until she found something that really worked, and then she used the Thomas Register to find U.S. manufacturers. She wrote, emailed and called the leather manufacturers listed, but all to no avail. Either it was too costly, the manufacturers didn't have the resources, couldn't meet the timelines or they did not work with small projects. Greenfield had to take her product overseas.

She found an independent sourcing consultant, Edith Tolchin, and started contacting Chinese manufacturers. Greenfield was concerned about finding a reputable manufacturer and made sure to do a lot of shopping around to find one that could really meet her needs. Her product needed to have a sleek, fashionable look and poor workmanship would kill the business. She made sure to ask all of the questions listed in this chapter and didn't commit to a manufacturer until she got good answers so she would know that she had a flexible, reliable supplier creating her wallots™ -- www.wallots.com.

Inventor Story:

Can You Make My Product?

John Shoenhair of Strategic Solutions is a home martini maker. His brother-in-law was telling him about how to make the perfect martini and he realized that something was missing in the process to really make it easy. After spending a few months of product development, Shoenhair applied for a patent for his new martini glass.

Shoenhair spent about a year unsuccessfully trying to license the idea and decided to try to start selling the product on his own. He searched for U.S. manufacturers, but found no one did the high quality, hand blown crystal he needed. He used some companies that try to connect entrepreneurs with overseas manufacturers, but even then only one or two companies could be found, and they were much too expensive. Shoenhair decided to look on his own.

After searching on the internet, Shoenhair compiled a list of potential manufacturers and found one that responded quickly to his requests and offered reasonable quotes. The deal sealer was that they also had a good line of similar products that gave Shoenhair the confidence that they could deliver his martini glass at the quality he needed.

Chapter 6

Placing a Purchase Order, Payment and Shipping Terms

You've been corresponding with a factory in China who has sent you great counter-samples and who has even made some suggestions to improve your original prototype. You are ready to place an order, and will jot down a few items you require, such as quantity, price, etc. You will e-mail these items in an informal purchase order to your new supplier, and everything will be ok, right? Wrong!

For your protection (and that of your new start-up business venture), make sure a properly written purchase order is drawn up. This is a contract between you and the Chinese manufacturer. Include buyer / seller names and addresses, phone/fax numbers, e-mail addresses, quantities, unit pricing (determine in advance if you will be paying "FOB China" pricing, which WILL NOT include ocean freight and marine insurance, or "CIF USA" port pricing, which WILL include freight and insurance – see sidebar for the "13 Incoterms"), payment terms, shipping terms, mold / tooling charges, and wire transfer details such as percentage for down payments (usually 30% down). Also include your list of production testing (as determined in your Design Evaluation, as mentioned in Chapter 2), where it will be done, Consumer Product Safety Improvement Act regulations, and who is paying for the tests. The most important item to incorporate into your PO is a STIPULATION FOR DEFECTIVE MERCHANDISE. Under a "comments" or "remarks" column in the POs I issue on behalf of my clients, I write, "Seller (name) is responsible for defective merchandise. Seller will be responsible for the entire cost of merchandise, freight charges for return of defective items, to be returned to the seller, in addition to replacement of the defective merchandise OR refund of buyer's payment (in U.S. dollars, at the option of the buyer, via Wire Transfer.)" Also provide all specifications, product description, components, Customs information (to be discussed in Chapter 7), and Import Security Filing information (ISF - to be discussed in Chapter 9), labeling and production testing (both in accordance with your Design Evaluation report), packaging information, carton marks, and international shipping documentation requirements, including the General Conformity Certificate – see Chapter 3 - which you will be responsible for.

For purchase orders, the more info you provide, the more protection you hold, and your supplier will not be able to say, "Oops! You never mentioned that!"

An important set up of terms to know are called Incoterms 2000, which is a list of international rules for interpreting the most frequently-used trade terms in international commerce. It consists of a series of 13 three-letter abbreviations.

The 13 Incoterms

Departure Terms

EXW – Ex-Works, lists the location where the shipment is available to the buyer, often location of the seller. Buyer assumes all responsibility for the product at pickup and arranges for all transportation.

Main Carriage Unpaid

FCA – Free Carrier: seller arranges and pays for transportation to the buyer's freight carrier, who then takes charge of the product at buyer's expense.

FAS – Free Alongside Ship: only for ocean shipments, the seller delivers shipment to the dock named by the buyer, after which the buyer arranges and pays for the remaining transportation.

FOB – Free On Board: only for ocean shipments, the seller delivers shipment to the dock and loads it onto the vessel named by the buyer, after which the buyer pays for the remaining transportation.

Main Carriage Paid

CFR – Cost and Freight, only for ocean shipments: the seller delivers shipment to the dock, loads it onto the vessel and prepays for shipping.

CIF – Cost, Insurance and Freight, only for ocean shipments: the seller delivers shipment to the dock, loads it onto the vessel, prepays for shipping and includes a marine insurance policy.

CPT – Carriage Paid To: the seller arranges and pays for shipment to a named destination.

CIP – Carriage and Insurance Paid To: the seller arranges and pays for shipment to a named destination and provides insurance for the shipment.

Arrival

DAF – Delivered At Frontier: for delivering to a land frontier, the seller arranges and pays for shipment to a named location, not unloaded and not cleared for import – meaning before the Customs border.

DES – Delivered Ex-Ship: only for ocean shipments, the seller arranges and pays for shipment to a named port, not unloaded and not cleared for import.

DEQ – Delivered Ex-Quay: only for ocean shipments, the seller arranges and pays for shipment to a named port, unloads the shipment onto the wharf, but does not clear the shipment for import.

DDU – Delivered Duty Unpaid: the seller arranges and pays for shipment to a named location, not unloaded and not cleared for import.

DDP – Delivered Duty Paid: the seller arranges and pays for shipment to a named location, not unloaded, but cleared for import.

The two most frequently used shipping terms when doing business with China are: "FOB" as in "FOB Shanghai", which means that the unit price being paid does NOT include ocean freight or marine insurance, which are to be arranged by the buyer via their freight forwarder or directly with the steamship company. "CIF", as in "CIF Miami", means that the unit price being paid to the China supplier will include COST, INSURANCE (usually marine insurance) AND FREIGHT (usually OCEAN freight), prepaid and arranged by the China supplier.

Payments

International purchase orders are usually paid by either Letter of Credit or wire transfer. As mentioned in Chapter 5, Letters of credit are used more often for larger quantity orders because of high fees and charges for discrepancies. The most widely used form of payment is a Wire Transfer, which means that money is transferred from your USA bank to the overseas supplier's bank. Typically a 30% down payment is placed by wire transfer to enable the supplier to purchase the raw materials necessary to begin production. After production is completed and all samples are approved (we'll get to quality control in Chapter 8), the 70% balance is paid by wire transfer

ONLY after the supplier presents you with a copy of the ocean or air shipping document as proof of shipment.

Inventor Story:

The Importance of a Purchase Order

When Maureen Howard's first child was six months old, he was not napping well. Only if he was wrapped warm and tight would he sleep better. Howard wanted to create an easier way to keep her son warm and snug and she created a homemade prototype of her Magic Sleep Suit, www.magicsleepsuit.com, which worked so well that she decided to turn it into a product and sell it.

Howard realized that she couldn't afford to make her product in the U.S. and was referred to Edith Tolchin. They found a manufacturer in China and started getting ready for production, but then some problems arose and for about six months they lost the manufacturer.

Howard decided to reconnect with the manufacturer and see what happened. Once she found out the issues, they were able to come to a mutual agreement to move forward. Howard ended up paying more per unit, but it was worth the additional costs because the cost to change to a new manufacturer would have been much greater. Additionally, she had already lost valuable time, and did not want to start all over again.

Once the manufacturer and Howard were on the same page, they signed a revised Purchase Order to document the changes in their agreement. With this new PO, Howard was confident that the manufacturer would honor their side of the new agreement and if any problems arose, she had a legal document to fall back on.

Chapter 7

US Customs and Border Protection Issues

So, you have determined that offshore manufacturing is the best solution for bringing your invention to market, right? Able to stick to the tight "start-up" budget for your newly formed business because you have now seen that it is very frequently cheaper to make your product in another country? The quality of the counter-samples you have been receiving from the various prospective sources is excellent – just as good as, if not better than those you had received from domestic factories?

Excellent quality counter-samples, cheaper costs, the Internet, which brings the entire world to your fingertips – you've done your preliminary research! Now what? When the factories have completed production, independent testing labs have performed their magic, you and your international trade consultant have "dotted all I's and crossed all T's," and you are ready to have your first order shipped - HOW MUCH IN IMPORT DUTIES WILL YOU BE PAYING FOR YOUR INVENTION???

IMPORT DUTIES – What!? Why!? How!? Have you ever traveled abroad and made some neat purchases of gifts and goodies that you haven't, or couldn't have found at home? You know that, when you return to the USA from a foreign country, you will have to go through Customs (formerly U.S. Customs Service – now called, "Customs & Border Protection, div. of the U.S. Dept. of Homeland Security"). If you have purchased over a certain dollar value of these items (depending on which country you visited), they must be declared with the Customs inspectors, and you must pay duty on the amount in excess of the allowed merchandise value (keep receipts)! Did you think that when you import your great new invention into the shores of the good ole' USA it would be any different? YOU MUST STILL PAY DUTY ON THE MAJORITY OF PRODUCTS IMPORTED INTO THE USA.

How do we find out how much duty you must pay on your soon-to-be imported invention? The two options are, first, to comb through the quite lengthy tome entitled the "Harmonized Tariff Schedule of the United States," published through the U.S. International Trade Commission. The "HTS" consists of two very detailed logs, the size of two Manhattan (NYC) phone books, with duty classifications for every product "under the sun", from animals, to fireworks, to raincoats, to computers parts! This guide can also be obtained online, but here's the catch: you must know what to look for! And, since the "HTS" shows duty classifications for "established" products, WHERE EXACTLY DO YOU CLASSIFY YOUR NEW INVENTION? Since most inventions are NEW ITEMS, chances are they won't be listed in the "HTS"! Sure, there may be a similar category – for example, you invented a special type of towel with unique pockets and other fabulous features. Do you look under Chapter 52-"Cotton" or under Chapter 63-"Other made up textile articles?" Good question, right? If you look into any of these chapters, there are so many different options – headings, subheadings, etc. - that after just a minute of reading through them, your brain begins to do a flashdance, out of synch, with your eyes! Again, since your product is unique – that's why it's called an invention – it is very difficult for a first-time importer to determine what the proper classification is for his/her product, in order to determine the duty amount to be added to their "landed" costs. What do you do next?

The old Greyhound commercial stated, "leave the driving to us!" Here is your second option: I recommend you ask your international trade consultant (I think every inexperienced prospective importer should work with one!) or licensed customs broker to prepare a request for a Customs **_Binding Ruling_** for your product. The Binding Ruling serves as protection for you, the importer. A sample (prototype is fine) of your invention, along with any literature you have available such as specification sheets, sales literature or brochures, packaging samples, labels, component information, etc., are sent to Customs, with a letter describing the ultimate use of your product, information about your company (to be called the "Importer of Record"), the manufacturer (if known at the time of ruling request), terms of sale, the ports through which you plan on importing the shipment(s) and any other information you or your representative feel may assist Customs in properly classifying your product.

WHY BOTHER? An example I always use is: your first shipment is due into port and is presented for customs clearance. Customs assigns a 5% duty rate and clears your shipment. You have paid 5% on the cost of your product. So, if the documentation shows that your product value was $10,000, the duty you paid was $500. About 6 months later, your invention has been very successful and this time you are importing a shipment valued at $100,000! You have budgeted the duties to now be $5000 (5%), right? WRONG! Without a Binding Ruling on a new invention with no other similar products listed in the "HTS," classifications (determination of import duties) are subject to interpretation by Customs at time of import. Another Customs Inspector who reads your shipment documentation this time may feel that the classification would carry an 8% duty rate. You are now paying $8000 even though you had budgeted only $5000 in duties! So, how do we avoid the "3 Gs" – (Gambling Guessing Game)??? Now you've got it right: A ***BINDING RULING***!

Why is this important? Improperly classified merchandise can carry very steep penalties! Your first shipment will take at least 45-60 days and US Customs will review the product and classify it within 30 days after receipt of sample. Since you have time anyway, you should take this very helpful precaution. Customs will even return your prototype if you wish, they will provide you with the duty rate, and even address international labeling and marking issues if you request this information. Proper labeling of your product and marking of your export cartons are also important to help avoid the possibility that your shipment may be detained for improper marking and/or labeling upon arrival in the USA. Penalties can be steep. Later on, when your shipment arrives in the USA, a copy of this Binding Ruling is presented during customs clearance. US Customs likes when you make it easy for them! So, to paraphrase another old saying, "it's not nice to fool Mother Customs!" Do it right from the very start, and you will have the satisfaction of knowing what you'll pay in import duties for all forthcoming shipments for your wildly successful "baby!"

Here are some important things to consider are if you want to employ a Customs broker and/or a freight forwarder. Freight forwarders are shipping companies who arrange your shipment, in the case of importing, typically from the overseas country into the USA, via air or ocean. Customs brokers are companies (or individuals) who hold US customs broker licenses. They are permitted to clear your shipment (whether via air or ocean) when it comes into the US Customs territory (i.e. USA port), and thereby import the shipment on your behalf, with your signed Customs Power of Attorney form. They will prepay duties, prepare necessary documentation, and then deliver the shipment to your inland delivery destination.

If you have never imported before, it is wise to use a Customs Broker, who will guide you through all the steps necessary to legally import your shipment into the USA. You can obtain a recommendation via someone who has imported before, or you can contact the National Customs Brokers & Forwarders Association of America, Inc. at www.ncbfaa.org.

Inventor Story:

The News Might Be Bad, But At Least You'll Know

Maureen Howard (from Chapter 6), with the assistance of Edie Tolchin of EGT Global Trading, applied for a binding ruling for her Magic Sleep Suit. Her product is in a new category, so she didn't know what kind of import duties she would need to pay. It turns out that the duties were much higher than she expected, but now at least she knows and can plan for the expense by figuring it in to her final product price.

Chapter 8

Quality Issues, Safety and Production Testing and Product Liability Insurance

Every product should have product liability insurance, especially products manufactured in China. Take examples of recent Product Recalls from the (US) Consumer Product Safety Commission,

Many large insurance companies provide business product liability insurance. A good product liability insurance provider is marshallandsterling.com.

www.cpsc.gov/cpscpub /prerel/prerel.html, for lead levels in children's toys from China. Independent safety testing via a CPSC-accredited lab is THE LAW, and should be done in conjunction with product liability insurance. Your insurance provider may give you some guidelines for product testing, but if not, it is far better to have your product safe from the start and go above and beyond to ensure your product is as safe as possible. If your product gets labeled as "unsafe", your image may be ruined forever, even if you make all the necessary changes to make the product safe.

Let's say that mass-production of your order is almost completed and your product has passed all of the production tests that were recommended in the Design Evaluation from the independent safety lab, as indicated in Chapter 2. The tests that you have chosen should have all been done at this point. Samples of production testing are: colorfastness, seam strength, flammability, shrinkage and toxicity in packaging. The tests should be done on a pre-determined number of actual mass-production samples to test for consistency in quality throughout the stages of manufacturing. You should have also approved all pre-production and mass-production samples, as part of the terms of your purchase order with the China factory. Your contact at the factory advises you that your order should be ready to ship in about 7-10 days. What should you do next? Order a *Final Shipment Inspection*!

Sure, the production samples that the factory sent you were good. And, they passed the safety tests. But how do you know that the shipment is consistent in quality throughout the numerous cartons, that it is packaged properly, and that your product has all of its components, labels, etc.? You need to have an inspection firm do a Final Shipment Inspection.

You should provide your desired inspection criteria for the firm's technician, including – if possible – photos showing "perfect" product vs. defective product, and even an actual sample of the product inside its packaging, with labels and all components. You may even give the technician a copy of the purchase order, which will clearly indicate shipping marks for cartons, labeling requirements, and so on.

A Final Shipment Inspection can be done by an inspection firm in China, such as KRT Audit Corporation, chinainspect.com.

The technician schedules an appointment with the China factory, performs the inspection in accordance with your desired criteria, and AQL (Acceptance Quality Level) in accordance with the ISO (International Organization of Standards).

In a very short time, you are provided with the Final Shipment Inspection report, which will be very thorough, and will include photos and comments on every aspect of your shipment. If there are any problems – and if you have allowed enough time – you may contact your supplier to make any necessary changes prior to shipment, either by e-mailing on your own, or by sending the technician's photos and/or even sending a copy of the Final Shipment Inspection report.

You can never be too safe with quality issues. Selling defective products will only do you harm; and, if you receive a shipment of bad products, even if your manufacturer is willing to replace entirely at its own cost, you will have lost valuable time and energy, either delaying the launch of your product or causing you to run out of inventory, thereby stalling sales efforts. Most retailers doubt inventors' ability to deliver products on time and consistently. Running out of inventory can cause you to lose hard earned retail accounts, so make sure everything is perfect before it leaves the factory.

Inventor Story:

Safety is a Number One Concern

Maureen Howard's (from Chapter 6) Magic Sleep Suit was a baby product in a new category; therefore there were no well defined safety standards. Because safety is vital for every product, and even more so for baby products, Howard wanted to take every precaution to ensure that when her product hit the shelves, there would be no safety concerns.

Howard, with the assistance of EGT Global Trading, found an international testing agency that first evaluated the safety of her design. They made suggestions to improve the product, which Howard incorporated into the final design. Then as the manufacturer was getting ready for production, she had the testing agency again test the pre-production samples to try to catch any other safety concerns.

While it is difficult to develop safety standards for a new product category, experienced CPSC-accredited testing agencies know what kind of red flags to look for and with their help, hopefully you will avoid a Product Recall from the CPSC.

Inventor Story:

What Kinds of Things Can Go Wrong?

Joe Yao, MD (from Chapter 1) has had some quality control problems with his Qwi™ Nerve Protection Gloves, http://www.qwinerveprotector.com. He does not employ an independent testing agency, but his manufacturer does provide him with a final quality control report on every shipment, plus sends production samples. Yao has already caught some problems based on the production samples, like the nerve pads in the wrong location, but there are more subtle problems that he was not able to detect.

A couple of times the manufacturer has substituted materials with disastrous results. The worst part is that the substituted materials looked so similar that Yao did not notice and the problem was only discovered when customers complained that the gloves were falling apart.

Yao's manufacturer has replaced all of the defective merchandise, but selling poor quality products is never good for your image.

Chapter 9

You're Ready to Ship... Now What?

The Final Shipment Inspection went well. Your supplier is preparing the order for shipment. Your purchase order indicates whether it will be going via ocean or via air. If, for example, it will be a prepaid ocean shipment (or in this case the shipping terms are "CIF New York" – which includes **C**ost, **I**nsurance and **F**reight to the port of New York), then the factory makes the arrangements with their China freight forwarder for your order to be placed on a vessel (or on an airplane for air cargo shipment).

Note that Customs and Border Protection (www.cbp.gov) has issued a new law, which took effect in 2010, called ISF (Import Security Filing). Simply put, certain specific information must be presented to Customs, usually arranged by your customs broker in the USA, in an "ISF" form, at least 24 hours before the shipment is loaded on a vessel. The information will include Seller and Buyer info, Importer of Record number (check with your customs broker), the Consignee Number, the "Ship to" party, Country of Origin of the product, and the product's HTSUS (Harmonized Tariff System of the United States – which is discussed under "Binding Rulings" in Chapter 7). Also required is the Container Stuffing Location, and Consolidator information.

Note that YOU, the Importer, are responsible for all information provided on the ISF form. Make certain that your China factory is aware of all of the data that is required for you to complete a properly executed form, far in advance of sailing – and this information should be included in your Purchase Order so there are no surprises. Violation of ISF can result in penalties in the thousands of dollars, issued by Customs and Border Protection.

For additional information, on ISF filing, please go to: http://www.cbp.gov/xp/cgov/trade/cargo_security/carrie rs/security_filing.

Once all arrangements are made, the factory will then send you a copy of the shipping manifest, dock receipt or cargo receipt as proof of shipment. At that point, you would issue a wire transfer payment for any balance due the supplier, which is typically 70% of the order value (if you have already sent, for example, a 30% down payment via wire transfer when your order was first placed). Your supplier will give you an ETA (estimated time of arrival) into your designated USA port, and will forward all necessary shipping documents, again – as stipulated in your purchase order, on to you, or your USA customs broker directly. It will be up to you or your consultant to contact the customs broker to send a copy of the Binding Ruling (as previously mentioned in

Chapter 7 – to determine import duties), so that the broker will properly classify your product, clear your shipment at your designated USA port, prepay any import duties, and ship it from the port to your warehouse or other inland delivery destination.

In the case of "FOB" (Free On Board) shipping terms, where you are responsible for the ocean freight and marine insurance, you can go to Customs & Border Protection's website (www.cbp.gov) for a list of Customs Brokers in the USA. (In this case, you must pay for ocean freight and marine insurance, instead of having these costs added to your unit cost from your China supplier, and prepaid and arranged by them.)

Contact a few of these Customs Brokers and they will give you the names of some freight forwarders they work with in China. When your supplier gives you the total number of cartons, volume and weights for your upcoming shipment, (also make sure the commodity is properly described on the documentation, such as 'shoes,' 'mugs,' 'baby toys,' etc.), the freight forwarder in China can give you a quote on the ocean freight and marine insurance, and they can also coordinate the collection of your order from the China factory when it is ready to go.

As previously mentioned, however, it's frequently less expensive to book a purchase order with "CIF" shipping terms, where ocean freight and marine insurance are prepaid by the China factory, because they often receive cheaper freight rates when all of this is arranged within China. You can also contact the National Customs Brokers & Forwarders Association of America, Inc. (www.ncbfaa.org) for further assistance.

Your consultant or your customs broker should inspect the international shipping documentation provided by the supplier, such as the commercial invoice, packing list, bill of lading, Certificate of Inspection, Marine Insurance Certificate, etc. to make sure all proper Customs information is included, that the product is properly described, and quantities and costs are correct. Just as with your purchase order contract, it is always better to have more information than less in international shipping paperwork.

When your order reaches the USA port, your customs broker will clear your shipment through Customs on your behalf, prepay any import duties, and deliver it to your warehouse or other final delivery destination. This is where having a Customs Binding Ruling, as previously mentioned, helps to expedite the customs clearance process.

Once your shipment clears Customs, you will need to decide if you or your Customs Broker will pick up your freight at the port. Typically, Customs Brokers have connections with reasonably-priced trucking companies and if you decide to have your Broker arrange delivery to your warehouse, garage or directly to your customer, they will prepay the freight charges and add it to your final Customs Brokerage invoice. Or, if the shipment is small (i.e. a few cartons), you might want to arrange to pick up your shipment at the pier, when the Broker tells you it's ready and sends you a pick-up Delivery Order.

Chapter 10

China Sourcing Checklist

Below is a short checklist to be used as a quick reference to help make sure you haven't forgotten anything. This is a good list to review a few times during the sourcing process and it also will help you understand the flow and timing of all the steps you need to take.

1) **Product Design Evaluation**: As mentioned in Chapter 3, the Consumer Product Safety Improvement Act was created in 2008 with regulations that affect products whether produced domestically or overseas. Choose a CPSC-accredited lab to evaluate your product for all pertinent regulations, to provide a list of both mandatory and optional production testing. Then have key issues translated into Chinese or other language of your factory of choice.

2) **Sourcing**: Locating foreign sources, checking their references, obtaining product samples. Presenting your prototype(s) for production of first counter-sample and price quotation. Exploring the possibility of locating an overseas buying agent (not applicable in all cases) who coordinates all transactions with the manufacturer, for a small commission (usually 2-4% of F.O.B. cost of item). Present prototype sample to U.S. Customs for "verbal

decision", or "Binding Ruling", on import duty/tariff rate, as well as for any special documentation requirements.

3) **Means of Financing the Import**: Upon determination of product cost, negotiation with vendor/agent regarding method of payment, i.e., wire transfer (the most widely used method), cash in advance (not a good idea), or letter of credit, usually used on large volume, high value orders. Locating an international bank to establish a credit line (for letters of credit).

4) **Sales contract**: Usually, a "Purchase Order". The first purchase order with a new vendor should be reviewed by your attorney or international trade consultant, if at all possible. Then a "sample" PO should be e-mailed or faxed to vendor/agent for their comments and review. All details must be included, such as method of shipment (air or ocean), inspections, special documentation, and especially proposed delivery dates. (This is VERY IMPORTANT, since foreign deliveries are RARELY on schedule). Finalize PO, sign, e-mail and/or mail original to vendor.

5) **Letter of Credit**: (If applicable) After credit line is established with bank, application is completed (not signed) and faxed on to vendor/agent for comments, review. Once this is done, Letter of Credit can be opened. Again, as mentioned above, this is usually for POs of very high value. Typically, wire transfers are sufficient for first orders, as previously discussed.

6) **Customs Brokerage/Power of Attorney**: A customs broker is appointed who will handle the customs entry/clearance process of the import transaction. A "power of attorney" form is sent to you to enable you/your company to be the "Importer of Record," and gives the customs broker your P.O.A. to clear your shipments. Single-entry or Continuous Import Bonds are determined at this stage, and your customs broker will arrange this for you.

7) **Production**: Goods are then produced in the factory. Weekly expediting details must be provided, which give you the production/delivery status of your product. Production samples are sent to importer for approval. At this point, towards the end of production, if you wish, you may request daily delivery progress updates. Production and Consumer Product Safety Improvement Act testing should be arranged, in accordance with the Design Evaluation (DE) you've had with your independent safety / testing lab, if applicable.

8) **Shipment:** When goods are ready, you must advise the vendor/agent the method of shipment you will use. Since you have plenty of time during the production process, you can research the most economical freight rates. Marine Insurance should be opened at this time, if applicable. All of this depends on the shipping terms of your PO, whether (for example) FOB China, or CIF USA port, as previously mentioned. Remember to work with your (USA) customs broker to make sure the Import Security Filing (ISF) Form is presented to Customs at

least 24 hours before your shipment is loaded onto the vessel.

9) **Payment**: If "wire transfer", vendor must meet all documentation requirements, then wire transfer is effected. If Letter of Credit, vendor and agent now work together to make sure ALL DOCUMENTS are presented to their (foreign) bank in a timely fashion (usually no later than 7-10 days). Photocopies of these documents are IMMEDIATELY faxed or e-mailed to you for your review. Foreign bank transmits documents to your bank for L/C negotiation. Bank notifies you of any discrepancies, which you must review. Your account is debited for the amount of the commercial invoice, and any applicable bank fees. YOU NOW OWN THE GOODS. Vendor then receives his payment from his bank. Original documents are then sent to you for:

10) **Customs Clearance**: Original shipping documents are sent to local customs broker (usually at the port where goods enter the U.S.), along with a letter of instructions, indicating where goods are to be delivered, once cleared by Customs. You determine method of shipment of the goods from the pier (or airport if it is an air shipment). If you use your own truck, trucker must be given a delivery order. If you use the customs broker's truck, you must advise them where to send the goods from the port (i.e. to your warehouse, directly to a customer, etc.) Clearance/entry is effected and import duties are prepaid. Customs broker sends you an invoice for these charges.

Chapter 11

How to Protect Your Product Idea

Overview

As defined by U.S. law, trademarks, servicemarks, copyrights, and patents are "intellectual property." In contrast, a car is considered "personal property," and a house and its land are considered "real property." For real property and personal property, what is owned can be seen and touched. What is owned as intellectual property can only be defined by words.

The Benefit of Patents

Inventors frequently ask Don Debelak, "how important is a patent?" His stock answer is that its importance is totally dependent on the value placed on a patent by the person with whom you are dealing. Don Debelak's experience is that in China, the manufacturers you deal with consider a patent important and place a high value on it. One can argue about whether a patent is weak or strong, but the fact is most people, especially overseas, expect you to have a patent and not having one can work against you. Whether the patent is strong or weak may be argued in the US, but overseas, people don't seem to try and evaluate if claims are broad or weak. What does count is having a patent.

Patent Searches

A "search" means looking at patents, magazines, product brochures, newspapers, and any written publication for information about what has already been thought of in the area or field of your **product**. When these written publications are found, they are called the "prior art." Prior art can be in a foreign language, and it doesn't have to be found in the United States or be easily available. Anything that is found may preclude getting a patent, and there is no differing level of importance among types of prior art; a magazine article can be just as meaningful as a prior patent. Inventors should realize that prior art that is searched will be less than half of the worldwide prior art, and that the U.S. patent examiner will see less than half of the worldwide prior art. That means that any patent issued by the USPTO may be found invalid later if better prior art is found, or if a company looking to copy your product can find previously unfound prior art.

Types of Patents:

Utility Patents

The patent that gives the longest protection and is the most common patent inventors receive.

Definition: Utility patents cover new methods of doing something, new devices for doing something, and new chemical compositions. A method of advertising, a method of washing clothes, and a method of making a product can be patented—as can a device that holds advertising, a device that washes clothes, a machine for making a product, and equipment for producing a paint remover.

Requirements: The product must be novel (new) and unobvious (a new combination that a person skilled in the field would not have thought of). For example, a Post-It note has an adhesive that sticks to the note but easily peels off from the next note in the stack of Post-Its. The paper for the Post-It note is specially designed to do this, and that paper formula would not be obvious because that feature had never been seen before.

Advantages/Disadvantages: The main advantage is that you have an intellectual property right that can be enforced to stop your competitors from copying your method or device and which can be licensed or sold to others. Many companies that license products require you to have a utility patent. A patent also offers benefits in the marketplace, as people in the distribution channel and end users tend to perceive patented products as having more value. Some disadvantages are that a patent may not prevent competition, it is expensive, and there is no one to enforce a patent except the patent holder. Stealing an idea is a subject for civil courts and not criminal prosecution.

Design Patents

Design patents offer a low cost, but with correspondingly low protection approach to getting a patent

Definition: The design of an object—its shape or ornamental look—can be patented. Some examples are a car fender, a soap holder, and computer housing, such as the design of Apple's iMac computer.

Requirements: The design must be different from what has previously been done (as established by prior art). This can be a very arbitrary decision, but almost all design patents are approved.

Advantages/Disadvantages: The main advantage is that you now have an intellectual property right that you can enforce, license or sell. You can place "patent pending" on the product as soon as your application is accepted, and you no longer need to have confidentiality agreements signed. The main disadvantage is that any minor changes in what is shown in the drawings of your patent may be enough to allow the competition to design around your patent.

Provisional Patents

Buys you one year of time before you submit your formal patent; also gives you foreign patent rights.

Definition: Provisional patent applications are never examined, meaning that no one reads them, and they allow you one year to submit a regular utility patent. The provisional patent was originally created to protect U.S. inventors' foreign patent rights. U.S. patent law gives you one year to apply for a patent after you start selling your idea, while foreign patent law requires that you obtain a patent before any sales efforts or any publicity is released. Cost varies depending on the complexity of your idea.

Requirements: The application must explain in words and drawings everything about your product. Photographs can be photocopied onto paper and included; however, a drawing of what is shown in the photograph should be provided. The application will be examined when you submit your official utility patent to make sure they are the same, and then the filing date of the provisional application will be used if there is a future patent dispute or if the patent office needs to decide whom to give a patent to when two similar patents have been filed.

Advantages/Disadvantages: One main advantage is that you can do the provisional application yourself, and it is a very low cost alternative to a regular application. It is considered a reduction to practice because, similar to making a prototype, you have proved the product will work; you no longer need to use confidentiality agreements; and you can place "patent pending" on the product or method. It is a useful tool even if you never intend to apply for a utility patent, as it offers patent pending status for one year, and this should allow you enough time to evaluate the commercial potential of your product. The main disadvantage is that you are required to file a utility patent application within 12 months or forfeit your ability to patent the idea.

Other Tactics:

Confidentiality Agreements and Nondisclosure Statements

Definition: This agreement goes by many names, but it is an agreement between you and another party (or person) not to disclose to a third party what you have shown them concerning your product.

Requirements: Some type of signed written statement where the person receiving confidential information agrees not to disclose the information to others.

Advantages/Disadvantages: The main advantage is that a confidentiality agreement makes the information you share with the other party a nonpublic disclosure under U.S. patent law, which in many cases protects your patent rights. Using such an agreement shows a very careful and businesslike approach to your dealings. The biggest disadvantage is that the agreement can't be enforced against a third party who learns from the signing party of your idea. Further, enforcement of the agreement against the signing party requires the filing of a lawsuit.

Inventor's Notebook

Definition: This is simply any kind of bound notebook—preferably one with numbered pages. If the pages are not numbered, number them yourself; this is done to show that no new pages were inserted at a later date. The engineering notebooks or accountants' ledgers sold in office supply stores are ideal.

Requirements. This should contain evidence of your activity—everything that you do should be entered into the notebook, in sequence, and dated. This includes drawings, ideas that you consider, and discussions with vendors and customers, along with the date and time of each event and notes on whether the interaction was in person or on the telephone. It should have a dated signature of one and preferably two people on each page with the notation, "The above material is confidential, and I have read and understood this page." Note: Have witnesses sign the book at least every week.

Advantages/Disadvantages: The main advantage is that it documents your product's progress and can be useful with potential partners and investors. It can also be useful in case you need to demonstrate the date that you first conceived your product and to show that the idea is indeed yours and that you didn't take it from someone else. The notebook can be easily kept up to date.

Patent Strategies:

Don't Bother

Explanation: If you don't need a patent to sell a product, you might want to avoid the expense if you are selling to a small market or if your product can't support a broad patent claim.

Advantages/Disadvantages: Basically, it costs nothing to do nothing, but you can't prevent competitors. Products without patents are probably impossible to license.

Patent Pending Strategy

Explanation: Once you have applied for a provisional, utility, or design patent, you can place "patent pending" on your product. The patent pending notice will scare away most companies from copying your product. One way to use this strategy is to apply for a low-cost design patent or a provisional patent without any intention of filing a final patent. On short-term promotional items, or fad items with a short life span, the patent pending status might be all the protection an entrepreneur needs.

Advantages/Disadvantages: There are a number of advantages: Many competitors will not try to introduce a competitive product to one that is patent pending.

Patent pending status is a better negotiating tool while getting a license, as the company won't initially know what your claims are. Patent pending status is almost as useful as an awarded patent when introducing a new product, and patent pending status can last for as long as 20 years if you keep changing your product's design. The main disadvantage: It doesn't provide any real protection for your product.

Low-Quality Patents

Explanation: Design patents and utility patents with narrow claims don't offer significant barriers to competitors, but they still have a deterrent value for some competitors, still offer a marketing advantage, and still help entrepreneurs license their ideas. Since the patent will have limited real protection, entrepreneurs can save money by patenting the product themselves. Patent It Yourself (Nolo Press) by David Pressman is an excellent resource for this. You can also proceed with a patent attorney.

Advantages/Disadvantages: A low-quality patent allows you to have the marketing and psychological advantages of having a patent, but it doesn't offer significant intellectual property barriers to competition.

Broad Patent with Few Specifics or Limitations

Explanation: A utility patent with a broad claim is worthwhile, and you should use a patent agent or attorney to file the application for you. This claim will help prevent competition and leave you in the best position possible to license your idea.

Advantages/Disadvantages: A broad patent offers strong protection from competitors and offers entrepreneurs a better chance of landing a licensing arrangement. The disadvantages are mainly monetary. As you proceed with the patent process, you may have numerous objections and rejections from the USPTO. It can easily cost $1,000 to $2,000 for each response to the patent office. You can end up spending well over $20,000—and in the end your final claim might be much more narrow than you expected, giving you nothing like the protection you had hoped for.

Many Weak Claims

Explanation: Sometimes products have close prior art that limits the scope of a patent. However, that prior art may not compete with the entrepreneur's product, nor may it diminish the novelty of the product to the marketplace. One solution to this problem is to file as many specific claims as possible in an effort to tie up every possible design. When done correctly, this tactic, in effect, gives the product a broad patent. This will require the filing of many applications and the costly prosecution of each application to issue.

Advantages/Disadvantages: This strategy can provide broad patent coverage for items unique to the market that have narrow patent claims due to prior art. A large number of patent claims discourages competitors and also provides a perceived edge in marketing the product. The disadvantage, again, is that it is an expensive process.

Foreign Patents

Filing for a U.S. patent only protects you in the United States. To protect yourself elsewhere, you have to file foreign patent applications. The "patent cooperation treaty" (PCT) application can be used to file your product in foreign countries that have signed the treaty.

The advantage of the PCT application is that you can file the same patent application in many countries. The disadvantage is that your patent rights can be 10 times more expensive than filing only in the United States. The total expense can be over $100,000 if you patent your product in the major countries of Europe and Japan. The violators of your patent rights will be more expensive to find. And the patent system and the courts that enforce the laws in foreign countries may favor their own citizens and companies over U.S. entrepreneurs.

Recommended Books

- The Copyright Handbook (Nolo Press) by Stephen Fishman
- License Your Invention (Nolo Press) by Richard Stim
- Patent, Copyright and Trademark (Nolo Press) by Stephen Elias
- Patent Searching Made Easy (Nolo Press) by David Hitchcock
- Patent It Yourself, 7th edition (Nolo Press) by David Pressman
- Trademark: Legal Care for Your Business & Product Name (Nolo Press) by Kate McGrath and Stephen Elias with Sarah Shena

Infringement Remedies

When a person or a company uses your trademark or service mark on their products or services or makes, sells or uses your patented device or method, the only option to stop them provided by law is to sue them. The cost of a lawsuit is very high, and usually both sides understand this. Many times, all that you—or your attorney—need to do is to write a letter to the offending party explaining the possible violation of your intellectual property right. Your letter should be phrased that there is a possibility the product or the method infringes the claims in your patent and that you would like to discuss the issue with them.

US Patent Considerations when Outsourcing to China

A U.S. patent protects you rights only in the U.S. One of the risks of outsourcing to China is that your manufacturer or another manufacturer might knock off your product. If that happens, what can you do? Patent law allows you to sue anyone who illegally violates your patent rights. That means you can sue a consumer, a distributor, a retailer, or even the manufacturer itself. Suing the consumers isn't practical or cost effective and you won't have much luck trying to sue the Chinese manufacturer in China, so you have to go after every retailer and/or distributor selling the knock-off. Sometimes a letter will have the retailer stop selling the knock-off, but that doesn't mean they will buy yours at a higher price. Unless you have established a market, preventing the knock-off from being sold doesn't really help you. Even worse, sometimes nobody stops selling the product and you have to go out and sue everyone, which will cost you a small fortune and you are by no means guaranteed a victory in court

Acknowledgements

The vast majority of the information in this appendix was provided by Albert W. Davis, davis al@msn.com, and Don Flickinger of Phoenix. Al Davis is a retired patent agent who has worked both independently with inventors and as an examiner with the U.S. Patent Office. Don Flickinger has worked for nearly 40 years as a patent agent. Both are found in the list of registered patent agents found at http://www.uspto.gov.

Inventor Story:

What Can You Do if Your Patent Doesn't Protect You?

In the late 90's, Steve Vetorino had an idea for a new flashlight, charged not by batteries, but by magnetic force from shaking the flashlight. He teamed up with Jim Platt and Todd Brown to bring the product to market. By 1998, their NightStar flashlight was being sold through catalogs and sales were steadily growing.

By 2001, a Chinese manufacturer created a knock-off that was selling for $15 less than the NightStar. Soon retailers and catalogs were dumping the NightStar in favor of the lower priced knock-off. Up until that time, the NightStar had been manufactured in Denver, but Vetorino, Platt and Brown realized that now they needed to move their manufacturing overseas so they could continue to compete.

They found a good Chinese manufacturer that produced high quality products and they started to implement some product changes. Since Vetorino, Platt and Brown had been selling the product for a few years, they had some ideas on how to improve it that they hadn't had the time, or the necessity, to implement. They realized that they couldn't compete on price alone, but if they had a reasonable price, they could compete on quality.

They took their beefed up product to a number of testing agencies for certification to work safely in a number of dangerous environments. They got all of these certifications which mean that their flashlight is purchased by organizations like the U.S. military, mining companies, and others who are concerned about safety.

Vetorino, Platt and Brown have used their certification as their marketing edge, aggressively attacking small markets where quality counts. There have been more than ten other knock-offs to enter the market and still the NightStar's sales continue to grow.

Vetorino has a patent, but that hasn't stopped competitors from entering the market. His patent isn't very strong, so Chinese manufacturers have found ways to design their products around his patent. Regardless, Vetorino, Platt and Brown have been able to stay one step ahead of the competition and continue to increase their sales every year. When standard intellectual property protection doesn't work, you need to use business savvy to stay ahead of the game.

Chapter 12

Helpful Links

1) Harmonized Tariff System of the United States- (for information on classifying your product for import duties):
http://www.usitc.gov/tata/hts/bychapter/index.htm

2) U.S. Customs and Border Protection- (for information on importing into the United States):
www.cbp.gov

3) Consumer Product Safety Commission:
www.cpsc.gov

4) Consumer Product Safety Commission's Accredited Safety Labs: http://cpsc.gov/cgi-in/labapplist.aspx

5) Consumer Product Safety Commission's Recalls and Product Safety News:
http://cpsc.gov/cpscpub/prerel/prerel.html

6) Consumer Product Safety Improvement Act:
http://www.cpsc.gov/about/cpsia/cpsia.html

7) Federal Trade Commission- (for information about labeling your products): www.ftc.gov

8) Federation of International Trade Associations:
www.fita.org

9) National Customs Brokers & Forwarders Association of America, Inc.: www.ncbfaa.org

10) KRT Audit Corporation- (for shipment inspections): www.chinainspect.com

11) Pantone- (for international color standards): www.pantone.com

12) Inventors Digest Magazine: www.inventorsdigest.com

13) United Inventors Association: www.uiausa.org

14) Ask The Inventors: www.asktheinventors.com

15) INPEX- (America's largest invention trade show): www.inpex.com - typically held once a year, in June, in Pittsburgh, PA.

16) Yankee Invention Expo: www.yankeeinventionexpo.org - typically held once a year, in October, in Waterbury, CT.

17) For shipping terms info: Incoterms 2000: http://www.uscib.org/index.asp?documentID=2213

18) INVENTOR MENTOR – Jack Lander: http://www.inventor-mentor.com

19) PROTOSEW – Barry Heim: http://www.protosew.com

Part 2: Marketing Wisely

Congratulations! Now you have a product to sell. How do you go about getting your product into the market? I've marketed over 30 new products and have developed a process to edge into the market and develop the contacts you need to succeed. At first I prepared a general article on setting up your distribution, one that would apply across all industries. But I realized that a general description wasn't that helpful for new marketers. Instead I've put together four chapters on how to sell to four markets often used by first time entrepreneurs: catalogs, the gift market, convenience stores, and finally carts and kiosks. You follow the same general steps in any market: first understand the market, attend shows, find reps or key buyers and then start selling.

Since many readers want to go after larger markets, the last two chapters deal with taking your product sales to the next level. First is a chapter about finding a marketing partner who can help you sell to major customers. This is the route you should travel when you sell to major retailers like Target and Best Buy for the first time. Get a partner who likes your product, is already in the big market, and can get you the market penetration you need for the first two years before you break off on your own. The last chapter involves what I feel is the most important key to success for a new marketer of an innovative product, finding key industry insiders who know what to do, already have key contacts, and are willing to help you succeed.

I wish you success in the market.

Don Debelak

Chapter 13

Selling to Catalogs

Mail order catalogs have long been one of the top ways for inventors to sell their products. Why is this? Catalogs don't mind taking products from one product companies, which is something avoided by many retail stores and distributors. But beyond that, catalogs can help you very effectively meet your sales goals and are often used as a launch pad for a new product. Catalogs can:

- Let you sell to a small market that can't be reached in any other way.

- Help you overcome retailers' reluctance to handle a product from a one-product company by proving that your product can really sell.

- Be your primary sales channel.

- Help you gain enough momentum for sales representatives to take your product on either for full- or part-time promotion.

Virtually any type of product can be sold through catalogs. Since most catalogs are aimed at specific niches, catalogs work best for inventors with specialty products. Products suited for catalogs usually have four characteristics:

1. They meet a need buyers already know they have. People skim catalogs and only notice products that catch their interest. That happens when the product meets a specific customer need.

2. They have a new or unique positioning statement. Most people think of products in categories. A consumer might see a new sleeping pillow and think it's just like the neck-bracing pillows sold in the past. Your product has to stand out in the market.

3. They are easily understood. You're lucky if readers even give your product a glance. Your invention needs to be understood in one to two seconds, or the prospect will move on.

4. They are priced appropriately for the catalog. Products priced from $12.95 to $29.95 do best in general-merchandise catalogs. Specialty and premium catalogs favor products priced from $40 to $500. Catalogers look carefully at how many dollars a product generates relative to the space it occupies on the page.

Find Your Target

Catalogs cater to specific audiences with a narrow product line. Levenger, for example, is a catalog of upscale products for serious readers. Find catalogs that sell to your target audience, sell products priced similarly to yours (economy, midrange, or premium), and sell products that are complementary to, but not the same as, yours.

Get a copy of each catalog, and look at the different products to find where yours fits. Double-check that each catalog's target market and pricing fit your product. Then make a list of the top 10 catalogs to which you will send presentation packages.

What to Send

You typically won't need to send a sample product. Catalogs often prefer to see a brochure or sales flier and price schedule first, then request a sample if they are interested in the product.

When you mail your package to the catalog company, include a mock-up of a typical page from the catalog that features your product alongside other complementary products already in the catalog. This shows the catalog buyer how your pricing and product features are a perfect fit.

Create a clear visual that lets people immediately connect to your product. This image can be of the product itself, or it can be of the situation the product solves. For example, a product picture of the dispensing racks that hold multiple drink cans in the refrigerator is easily understood by potential customers. But they may need a visual of a dandelion-removing tool in action to quickly understand how it works.

Match the style of copy on your sales materials to the style of each catalog. Many marketers who sell to various catalogs custom-write their materials each time. Having the right style helps persuade buyers that your product is perfect for their catalogs.

If you have any past publicity, include it in your presentation. If you don't have any, manufacture some. Host an event--it doesn't have to be big--that allows people to use your product, and then ask them to offer testimonials. For example, you could organize a 5-kilometer bike ride for 10 people to showcase a new, more comfortable bicycle seat.

How to Send It

When you send your package is just as important as what you send. Catalogs typically decide to buy products only once or twice a year, when they are laying out their new catalogs. Often, this date could be four to five months before the catalog is actually printed. Find out when a cataloger finalizes its product decisions, then mail to the catalog twice: two months before the final date, and again two weeks before the date. Mailing two months before will help get your product considered in the regular decision process. Mailing two weeks before the deadline puts you in front of catalog buyers right when they are trying to fill last-minute holes in the catalog.

Before sending your package, find out the name of the buyer for your type of product. If you call and ask, most catalogs will tell you. If you don't know who the buyer is, you won't know if your information reaches the right person, and you won't know who to call when following up.

Catalogs don't want products everyone else has. You can often get a foothold in the market if you tell buyers your product will only be in one or two catalogs the following year. This gives them a little more incentive to buy, and it allows you to ask the buyer for a response by a certain date so that you can contact other buyers if the first catalog doesn't want your product.

Is It Worthwhile to Sell Through Catalogs?

One of the biggest advantages of catalog sales is that you have few expenses other than manufacturing costs. There are minimal sales and marketing expenses, which in most other marketing channels consume 20 to 40 percent of your sales dollars. You will probably make money as long as you can sell your product for 50 percent more than your manufacturing cost.

The only major expense is that catalogers often ask you to pay part of the printing cost. This should be no more than 15 percent of your projected sales volume. If the printing costs are too high, you can frequently negotiate a better deal.

Interested in selling to catalogs? Check out Don Debelak's Catalog Marketing Program at selltocatalogs.com.

Tell the catalog you'll pay with free goods; for example, you'll include 15 percent extra merchandise with each shipment to pay for printing.

Many catalogs have gone out of business recently, and many more are operating on a shoestring. Ask for credit references and don't pay for printing before the catalog is printed; pay only in free goods or discounts off your invoice.

Sustaining Success

As a rule, catalogs change a substantial number of product offerings every printing. So unless your product is a top seller, you can expect to be dropped from a catalog every now and then. You can minimize the roller-coaster effect of catalog sales by creating strong relationships with buyers. Ask buyers what their goals are for the next issue and what you could do with your product to help them meet their objectives. You should also:

- Create variety. Catalogs don't like to have the very same products as other catalogs, so offer your product with several variations for catalogs to choose from. You can offer different colors or a few new features, or pair the product with different complementary items. A painting tool, for example, might come with a paint-can opener one season and a masking aid the next.

- Add catalog customers. You may have offered an exclusive contract to a catalog for the first year of catalog sales, but you can only grow your business by adding catalogs on a regular basis. Find new target catalogs, and keep going after them.

- Support the product. Your value to catalogs declines rapidly if you have quality or return problems. Most companies try to overcome this by directing product returns to themselves. Give consumers a toll-free number to call for questions and problems, and provide instructions on returning a product to you. You want to clear up every problem on your own to avoid conflicts with the catalog.

The drawback to catalog sales is that your product is exposed to a wide variety of people. Potential competitors can see your product, realize it has potential and decide to compete with you. You should at least have "patent pending" status before approaching catalogers, or you risk someone taking your idea.

Chapter 14

Selling into the Gift Market

Gifts can be sold in any number of stores, card shops, flower shops, drug stores, cooking stores, airport shops, Christian gift stores and hospital gift shops. Gifts represent an enormous product category, with products covering the gamut from home made sewing items to high tech widgets and gadgets. Though the stores are many and often small, the gift market is an attractive market for new product developers because they are sold through a well-oiled, and fairly easy to penetrate distribution channel. An additional advantage the gift market has is that new products can be sold locally, at a relatively low cost, until the new product developer knows the product will be a success.

The gift market distribution channel consists of gift shows, gift reps, gift marts and finally the store that sells the gifts. The distribution channel is expensive though and you need to be sure that you are able to sell your product at retail for about five times its manufacturing costs. The strategy most new product entrepreneurs follow is:

1. attend a few gift shows
2. attract the names of some reps with a presence in at least one gift mart

3. sell through the reps to the stores in his or her geographic area

Most people start in their local geographic area and then just keep expanding into new markets following the same introduction strategy.

Industry Magazines

As in any market, you need to start by getting copies of the trade magazines. They will have articles on distributors, distributor margins and the names of key trade shows and contacts that will help you determine your marketing strategy. They also typically have a yearly products directory that will help you understand what competition you are facing. The leading trade magazines for the gift market are:

1. Giftware News, 20 West Kinzie, 12 th Floor, Chicago, IL, 312-849-2220, Fax: 312-849-2174 www.giftwarenews.com

2. Gifts and Decorative Accessories, 360 Park Ave. South, NY , NY 10010 , 646-746-6400, Fax: 66-746-7431 www.giftsanddec.com

3. Giftbeat, 317 Harrington Ave. Closter, NJ 07624 , 800-358-7177, Fax: 201768-3894 www.giftbeat.com

Gift Shows

The gift industry has a large number of state wide and regional shows that you should attend, first if possible, as an attendee to see what the show is like, and second to meet sales reps. Most booths at these gift shows are run by sales representatives who carry a wide range of products. Almost all gift products from small manufacturers are sold through sales representatives (sales representatives that are independent business people and carry products from a number of manufacturers) and you need to start talking to them, hopefully finding one who will carry your line, or if that doesn't work out getting some insight into what they feel you might need to do to attract a sales representative to work on your product. Sales representatives will also help you set a realistic price, decide on the type of distribution discounts you need and determine the type of sales flyers you might want to prepare. (Note: you can also obtain this information if you order a marketing plan from onestopinventionshop.net.) You should also look for small entrepreneurs at the show who are trying to sell their products. They typically will tell you what they went through to get started in the industry and they will often provide you some start-up hints. At the end of this chapter there is a list of some of the more important gift shows that you can attend. When you approach the show they will usually resist letting you attend if you are not a buyer. You can ask for exception if you say you are in the process of starting a company that sells gifts and you want to see what the show is like. If that doesn't work, you can try to having a store that sells gifts in your area designate you as their representative to get into the show.

Gift Marts

Besides gift shows, the gift industry depends on gift marts to sell to retailers. Gift Marts have showrooms, typically run by independent sales representatives but sometimes run by companies, where store buyers can come and buy products. At the end of this section is a listing of most of the major gift marts. The showrooms are often open only by appointment, but the gift marts will offer special days, often once a quarter where all the showrooms will be open. If you are a buyer, or have a buyer's pass from a store that sells gifts you can see the showrooms and meet reps. But even if you can't get into the marts, they still can provide a valuable service in finding the names of representatives that you can approach to sell your product. To find the names of reps, start by going to the gift mart and go to a listing of the showrooms, many of whom will be representatives. For example, here is a sampling of names from the show room listing of the Seattle Gift Mart. This is a small listing, there are many more on their website.

ALAYNE GROTHEN & COMPANY - Suite 215
206-767-5720, 888-767-5722
Fax: 206-767-1707

E-mail: info@alaynegrothen.com
Open Mon-Thu; Design Trade Welcome

ARLENE OOM & COMPANY - Suite 291
206-762-3140, 800-228-5218
Fax: 425-649-0422; 888-892-0422
E-mail: toyrep@runbox.com
Open Mon & Tues, By Appt., Design Trade Welcome

ASSOCIATES MARKETING GROUP - Suite 375
206-762-1249, 800-775-6434
Fax: 206-762-2113
E-mail: assocmg@aol.com
Website: www.associatesmarketing.net
Open Mon & Tues
Design Trade Welcome

BANG-KNUDSEN, INC. - Suite 453
206-767-6970, 800-735-7241
Fax: 206-763-6985
E-mail: pbang-knudsen@bang-knudsen.com
Website: www.bang-knudsen.com
Open Mon-Fri
Design Trade Welcome
Open Mon & Tues

Using the list you can develop an extensive list of representatives that might be able to carry your product. You can also use this list to get a listing of representatives that might carry your product who don't have showrooms. If you click on the sales representatives web site you can find the names of the lines they handle. If you check the web sites of those manufactures somewhere between one out of five or 10 will provide a complete listing of all their representatives. You need reps to succeed in the gift industry and you should be able to generate a list of between 200 and 400 reps who could sell your product.

Gift Marts

Seattle Gift Mart

6100 Fourth Ave , South
Seattle , WA 98108
(206) 767-6800

Gift Center at Montgomery Park
2701 NW Vaughn Street
Portland , OR 97210
501) 228-7275

San Francisco Gift Center
888 Brannan Street
San Francisco , CA 94103
(415) 861-7733

Los Angeles Mart
1933 South Broadway
Los Angeles , CA 90007
(213) 749-7911

Denver Merchandise Mart
451 East 58th Ave.
Denver, CO 80216
(303) 292-6278

Kansas City Merchandise Mart
6800 West 115th Street
Overland Park , KS 66211
(913) 491-6688

Dallas Market Center
2100 Stemmons Freeway
Dallas , TX 75207
(214) 655-6100

Minneapolis Gift Mart
10301 Bren Road , West
Minnetonka , MN 55343
(612) 932-7200

Indianapolis Gift Mart
4475 Allisonville Road
Indianapolis , IN 46205
(317) 546-0719

The Merchandise Mart
Merchandise Mart Plaza
Chicago , IL 60654
(312) 527-4141

Columbus Gift Mart
1999 Westbelt Drive
Columbus , OH 43228
(614) 876-2719

Americas Mart Atlanta
240 Peachtree Street NW
Atlanta , GA 30043
(404) 688-8994

Charlotte Merchandise Mart
2500 Fast Independence Blvd.
Charlotte , NC 28205
(704) 377-5881

Mid Atlantic Gift Center
12260 Sunrise Valley Drive
Reston , VA 22091
(703) 391-0095

The Pittsburgh Expo Mart
105 Mall Blvd
Monroeville , PA 15146
(412) 856-8100

Market Center
230 Fifth Ave.
New York , NY 10001
(212) 686-1203

New York Merchandise Mart
41 Madison Ave.
New York , NY 10010
(212) 686-1203

The Northeast Market Center
1000 Technology Park Drive
Billerica MA 01890
(800) 435-2775

Miami International Merchandise Mart
777 NW 72nd Ave.
Miami , FL 33126
(305) 261-2900

Michigan Gift Mart

133 W. Main
Northville , MI
(313) 348-7890

Action Plan

A strategy that typically works in the gift industry has just four steps.

1. Sell first directly to a few local gift shops. If you have to you can put the product in on consignment, which means the gift shop won't pay you until the product sells.

2. Run promotions to help drive sales through those retailers. Momentum is important to sell to reps, you want to be able to show not only that the product is being sold in stores but that the product is selling out and stores are reordering. A great display can often be the best way to promote sales.

3. Attend a local gift show. Most of the gift marts will have certain days throughout the year where local manufacturers, including inventors, can set up a small booth to present their product to retailers. Be sure at these shows to have pictures of your product selling at the local retailers where you had sales success. Be prepared to offer goods on consignment or at a discount to get people started buying your product.

4. Once you have momentum including: a) success at certain retailers that have already reordered; b) attendance at a trade show or gift mart display day; and c) orders from retailers attending the show; then you are prepared to start doing a campaign of sending out mailings, doing follow-up phone calls and, when needed, sending out a sample of your product to have sales reps start carrying your products.

US and Canadian Gift Shows

ALASKA

The Wholesale Alaskan Gift Show,
www.newimpressions.com

ARIZONA

OASIS Gift Show, www.oasis.org

ARKANSAS

Eureka Springs Gift Show,
http://www.eurekaspringsgiftshow.com/default.htm

CALIFORNIA

California Gift Show, www.californiagiftshow.com

California Market Center,
www.californiamarketcenter.com

Gourmet Products Show, www.glmshows.com

IDEX (Collectible Doll and Bear Exposition),
www.dollexpo.com , www.bearexpo.com

International Gift Fair, www.weshows.com

LA Gift MART, www.lamart.com

Long Beach Furniture & Accessory Market,
www.kemexpo.com

NASFT Fancy Food Show, San Francisco,
www.fancyfoodshows.com

San Francisco International Gift Fair, San Francisco,
www.sfigf.com

CANADA

Alberta Gift Show, www.albertagiftshow.com

Canadian Gift and Tableware Association
http://www.cgta.org

Montreal Gift Show, www.montrealgiftshow.com

Vancouver Gift Show, www.vancouvergiftshow.com

Vancouver British Columbia , www.coffee-expo.com

COLORADO

Denver Merchandise Mart, www.denvermart.com

International New Age Tradeshow, www.inats.com

FLORIDA

Orlando Gift Show, www.orlandogift-how.com

IDEX (Collectible Doll and Bear Exposition),
www.dollexpo.com , www.bearexpo.com

International New Age Trade Show East, www.inats.com

Miami International Gift & Decorative Accessories Show,
and Miami Resort

Merchandise Show, Miami International Merchandise
Mart, www.urban-expo.com

Tampa Furniture & Accessory Market,
www.kemexpo.com

Orlando Variety Merchandise Show,
www.merchandisegroup.com

GEORGIA

ACC Craft Show, www.craftcouncil.org

Atlanta International Gift Market,
www.americasmart.com

The Gift Fair in Atlanta
http://www.thegiftfairinatlanta.com

HAWAII

Hawaii Trade Shows, www.douglastradeshows.com

ILLINOIS

ACC Craft Council Shows, www.craftcouncil.org

Beckman Handcrafted Show,
www.mmart.com/giftandhome

Chicago Gift & Home Market, The Merchandise Mart,
www.giftandhome.com

International Housewares Show, www.housewares.org

NASFT Fancy Food Show,
http://www.fancyfoodshows.com

St. Louis Gift Show, www.stlouisgiftshow.com

PromoExpo & Conference, www.promoexpo.com

INDIANA

Indiana Gift Mart; tel. 217/423-5185.

Heritage Cash and Carry Wholesale,
www.heritagemarkets.com

KANSAS

K.C. Gift Mart, www.kcgiftmart.com .

KENTUCKY

Kentucky Crafted, www.kycraft.org

Louisville Gift, Craft & Jewelry Show, www.louisvillegiftshow.com

LOUISIANA

New Orleans Gift and Jewelry Show, www.gift2jewelry.com

MAINE

New England Products and Trade Show, http://www.nepts.co m

MARYLAND

ACC Craft Show, www.craftcouncil.org

East Coast Gift Expo, www.urban-expo.com

MASSACHUSETTS

The Premier Show, www.thegiftcenter.com

The Cape Cod Gift Show, www.capecodgiftshow.com

Boston Gift Show, www.bostongiftshow.com

The Buyers Cash & Carry Wholesale Mart, http://www.marketsquareshows.com

Heritage Cash & Carry Wholesale Market, www.heritagemarketing.com

MICHIGAN

Michigan Gift Mart, www.michigangiftmart.com

MINNESOTA

Minneapolis Gift Mart, www.mplsgiftmart.com

MISSISSIPPI

Biloxi Gift Show, www.wmigiftshows.com

MISSOURI

St. Louis Gift Show, www.stlouisgiftshow.com

NEVADA

Las Vegas Souvenir & Resort Gift Show, www.urban-expo.com

Las Vegas Trade Show, www.merchandisegroup.com/merchandise/index.jsp

NEW JERSEY

Atlantic City Variety Merchandise Show, www.merchandisegroup.com/merchandise/index.jsp

NEW YORK

American Gift and Art Show,
www.westernnewyorkgiftshow.com

New York International Gift Fair, www.nyigf.com

225 Gift and Housewares Show, www.225-fifth.com

Upstate New York State Gift Expo,
www.upstatenygiftexpo.com

Variety Merchandise Show,
www.merchandisegroup.com/merchandise/index.jsp

West New York Gift Show,
www.westernnewyorkgiftshow.com

NORTH CAROLINA

Charlotte Gift Show, www.charlottegiftshow.com

OHIO

Columbus Gift Mart, www.columbusgiftmart.com

OKLAHOMA

Oklahoma City Gift Show, www.wholesalemarketinc.com

OREGON

Portland Gift Show, www.portlandgift.com

PENNSYLVANIA

Cash and Carry Wholesale Market,
www.marketsquareshows.com

Philadelphia Gift Show, www.urban-expo.com

Pittsburgh Gift Show,
www.westernnewyorkgiftshow.com

SOUTH CAROLINA

Grand Strand Gift & Resort Merchandise Show,
www.urban-expo

TENNESSEE

Norton 's Gatlinburg Gift and Variety Show,
www.ommart.com

Smoky Mountain Gift Show,
www.smokymtngiftshow.com

TEXAS

Dallas International Gift Market,
www.dallasmarketcenter.com

Houston Variety & Merchandise Show,
www.merchandisegroup.com/merchandise/index.jsp

San Antonio Gift Show, www.wholesalemarketinc.com

UTAH

Salt Lake Wholesale Gift Show, 801-566-9300

VIRGINIA

Washington Gift Show, www.washingtongiftshow.com

WASHINGTON

Seattle Gift Show, www.seattlegift.com

WASHINGTON DC

Greater Washington Gift Mart, 703-352-8010

Washington Gift Show, www.washingtongiftshow.com

Chapter 15

Distribute Your Product to Convenience Stores

Chapter also includes:

- Description of various organizations typically found in an inventor's distribution channel.

- Explanation of how to find a distribution channel for your product.

Many inventors have small novelty products where they want their products sold to convenience stores. This has been a difficult market for inventors because the distributors are typically rack jobbers who actually own the merchandise and buy at 40 to 45% of retail. The distributors can be hard to find as they don't have a Standard Industrial Classification (SIC) dedicated to them, and most operate on the office supplies distributor SIC code. (For more information on SIC codes go to http://www.siccode.com/about.php.)

Recently on a project though, I can across a great resource, Mr. Checkout, http://www.mrcheckout.net. According to the website description "Mr. Checkout is a national organization of (DSD) Direct Store Delivery Wagon-Jobbers, Distributors, Retail Merchandisers and Wholesale-to-Distributor Warehouses servicing

Convenience and Grocery Stores in the US since 1989. Our DSD / Full-Service Merchandising Distributor Members call on c-stores weekly." The site has a large number of services including a Walgreens merchandising program and a product placement blitz service. Everyone should check this site out if you have a product for drug stores, convenience stores or grocery stores. I can't vouch for the association but I did find the site had a great deal of helpful information.

Over the years I have found that inventors are unfamiliar with distribution, which is the channel that a product follows to take to market. Often products are handled by your own direct sales efforts, reps (also called manufacturers' sales agents), brokers, specialty distributors, wholesale distributors, other manufactures with complementary lines, and rack jobbers all who may play a role in selling a product. The path your product follows to market is called a distribution channel. For example you may sell a product through a rep to a rack jobber distributor who sells to convenience stores who then sells to the consumer.

Description of terms often used when discussing in the distribution channel:

Direct sales: Indicates that sales are handled by the selling company's own sales force.

Reps (manufacturers' sales agents): Independent contractors that promote a Company's line, but have very limited authority to commit a company to any but its standard sales terms. In effect a salesperson that represents a variety of companies with non-competing product lines. They typically call on a specific industry, and carry product lines where the sales volume isn't large enough to justify a direct salesperson. Reps don't take title on a product and work commonly on a 5% to 20% commission.

Brokers: Brokers are similar in some respects to a rep, they are independent from the companies they serve and receive a commission but they are more oriented towards the buyer than the seller. A rep will not carry competing lines and will have a wide range of products. A broker has a narrow range of products and many of them compete. An insurance broker, for example, carries lines of insurance from many companies, and will chose the company that is best for his customer. An insurance agent carries only one company's products, and tries to steer everyone to buy those products. A clock broker, for example, might have three stores as customers, and have access to many lines of clocks. He would then offer clock lines to his customers so they would have a constantly changing variety of clocks. Reps are far more common than brokers.

Private label: This is a practice where a company makes a product that it sells to another company that markets the product under their brand name. For example, a toy company might make a toy that is sold under the Toys R Us label. Or it might make a toy that is sold to Play School and then Play School would sell it under its label. Private labels sellers own the rights to the product and develop and produce the product to their specifications. Toys R Us might also develop toys that they have produced by a manufacturer. That manufacturer would be a contract manufacturer, rather than a private label manufacturer, because it didn't create the product and it doesn't own rights to the product.

Specialty retail distributors: Distributors serving small markets, for example baby stores or bike shops. These distributors take title to the product and promote the product and typically carry many products from one product inventor oriented companies. They are a key component in most inventor companies' distribution plans. They typical mark up (raise their price by) 35 to 40% before selling to retailers.

Industrial distributors: These companies typically sell directly to industrial companies, versus selling to a retail store. Graingers and Fastenall are examples of industrial distributors that sell a wide range of products to companies. You also have specialized industrial distributors. Some examples would be a pump and compressor distributors, a distributor that sell products for high temperature furnaces, or a company that supplies safety equipment. These companies typically have a high level of technical support to help chose the right products and then get the products to work effectively for them.

Trade distributors: These are distributors that deal with tradesmen versus industrial or consumer oriented accounts. Plumbing distributors, wood products distributors that sell to contractors, auto parts distributors that serve car repair shops are just a few of the types of distributors that sell to various trades.

Wholesalers: Wholesalers are also a distribution point between manufactures and their customers. While distributors provide promotion and service, wholesalers typically don't. They also rarely carry products from inventors as they purchase very large stocks of products and serve markets like grocery stores. Like distributors they take ownership of the product, but typically only mark the product up 15 to 20%.

Rack jobbers: Rack jobbers are a specialty type of distribution. Most distributors take title to the product and then sell It to a store or industrial company that takes title. Rack jobbers instead rent portions of a store, which might just be a section of a rack, or endcap positions at the end of the store aisles by the cash registers. Durable hair care products (brushes, combs and other product related hair care products) at drug stores are a typical rack jobber item. The rack jobber owns the merchandise in the store, replaces it and is only paid for the merchandise when it is sold by the store. Typically rack jobbers raise their purchase price 50 to 75% and then the stores mark the product up an additional 50%.

Selling through other manufacturers: One of the reasons companies use reps is that they don't have enough sales volume on their own to justify a direct salesperson. Those companies are often willing to pick up a line from another company if it puts them in a position to have their own direct sales force.

How to find agents and distributors.

One of the services offered at the onestopinventionshop.net is creating a list of distributors or manufacturers representatives. Finding the names of reps and distributors can be time consuming but it is something most inventors should be able to do on their own.

Step 1: Start by looking for trade associations, trade magazines and trade shows. You can find associations and trade magazines with internet searches if you are lucky, or by going to one of your larger libraries, where you can look for The Encyclopedia of Associations by Gale Research, and also Gale Research's Directory of Magazines and Broadcast Media. Both of these directories have a wide range of groups for even the smallest trade associations and trade magazines.

Once you find a list of associations and trade magazines you should go to their site and look for a list of manufacturers' representatives or distributors. For example I went to look for products for the baby industry in Gale's Encyclopedia of Associations. I found the association Juvenile Products Manufacturers Association. When I went to the web site, www.jpma.org, I found they had a list of manufacturers' sales agents. Often the web sites will also have a list of distributors, similar to the Mr. Checkout web site (www.mrcheckout.net).

Step 2: Develop a list of manufacturers in the industry. You can find lists of manufacturers in the trade association and the trade magazines web sites. Trade magazines will also have a list of trade shows. If you go to the web sites for those trade shows you can usually get a list of exhibitors. You can make the list more complete by using your library again. Most bigger libraries have a service called Reference USA in their online services. You can also use the service at home once you have the library password. Go to the site www.referenceusa.com before going to the library to see what information you will need. Then look up the SIC codes for a few companies on the site. SIC stands for Standard Industrial Codes, and typically most companies in the industry will have the same code. Once you have the SIC Codes you can do a search based on SIC codes and get a list of many of the companies in the industry.

Step 3: Go the web sites of companies in the industries. Some of the companies will list distributors, and others will list manufactures representatives. Other companies will be looking for representatives or distributors. Often it pays off to call those companies and see if they would like to partner with you in marketing your products. This is a tactic to consider because often manufacturers reps and distributors don't want to carry a line that is too small. You and your partner company might have enough volume together to entice distributors or manufacturing reps to carry your product.

You can also find representatives at the manaonline.org, which is the site of the manufacturers' agents' national association web site.

Success Tip

If you are a minority or women-owned business you might want to check out the site http://supplierregistration.target.com/Supplier/supplier_r egistration.aspx to get idea of the information you need to know to become a supplier for a leading store.

Chapter 16

Selling Your New Product through Carts and Kiosks

If you walk through any mall today you will see dozens of carts and kiosks, and you will see that number skyrocket as the Christmas season approaches. The market looks big and it is: $12.7 billion in the US alone. It is clearly a market that shouldn't be ignored.

While many of the Kiosks are from franchisers with a start-up package (approximately 300 top Cart & Kiosk packages are listed in the winter 2009 issue of Specialty Retail Report (www.specialtyretail.com), there is still a huge market for inventors to sell to independent cart and kiosk owners plus inventors can also sell to the franchisers of those kiosks systems. Both outlets offer strong sales opportunities to inventors with a unique product. The kiosks are particularly strong outlets for inventors that have products that work best with a demonstration and might otherwise be hard to sell in a store.

Probably the strongest reason to check out the Cart and Kiosk market is that those retailers operate from locations that give your product optimal exposure to the market.

Products that Work Best

- Price point should be between $10.00 and $150.00. Kiosks just can't carry enough low price inventory to generate the sales they need. They need a high priced product, $10.00 is the minimum and the $150.00 price is about as high as you can go for an impulse purchase.

- You need the suggested retail price to be two to three times the price you sell to Cart and Kiosk retailers. These retailers have to sell high priced products at a high margin to cover their costs and make money.

- The product is great for an impulse purchase. Carts and Kiosks make their living from a product that people see in a mall and can't resist from buying right then.

- The product demonstrates well. Cart and Kiosk retailers want to make a sale right then and now, and a great demonstration helps them do that.

- A minimum of 10 to 25% of consumers are potential customers. Cart and Kiosk vendors make money by attracting people who are passing by in the mall. Your product has to potentially appeal to a significant number of those people for the Cart and Kiosk retailers to make money.

How To Get Started

1. Start subscribing to the Specialty Retail Report (www.specialtyretail.com). It is a leading magazine for Cart and Kiosk retailers. It is also the best source for a list of franchises that sell Cart and Kiosk start-up packages.

2. Investigate the SPREE Show (www.SPREEshow.com) web site and consider visiting or exhibiting at the show. You can sell to both independent Cart and Kiosk vendors and franchisers at the show.

3. Visit many malls to get ideas for packaging and demonstrations. You also want to spend a long time studying very strong point of purchase displays. You need to offer many tools to Cart and Kiosk vendors so they can attract people to their location. Your packaging should be able to pull people over to the cart or kiosk from 20 to 50 feet away. You need strong visual graphics. Look for products that have strong visual appeal and use them as a starting guideline for your product.

4. Use the Specialty Retail Report Directory of Top Cart and Kiosk Start-up vendors to find franchisers who would be good sales candidates to approach.

5. Either start in the industry by attending the SPREE show, or start by contacting the franchises that you feel would do best selling your product. Be sure to have a strong package, point of purchase display, instructions for demonstrating your product and a price list before approaching companies for a sale.

Chapter 17

Selling Big: Finding the Right Marketing Partners

Once inventors have a product ready to sell, they need to decide how to market the product. They might choose to sell the product themselves, which generates the most profit per sale, but the main drawback is that sales might get off to a slow start or never get started at all. Another option is to land a marketing partner--another company already selling into the target market--which has the potential for very fast sales growth, but the main drawback is they will need to give 20 to 25% of their sales volume to the marketing partner to cover sales and marketing costs. At first glance the 20 to 25% seems high, but in reality most consumer products companies spend approximately 20% to cover sales and marketing costs. Selling through a marketing partner may not be viable if you have small margins, but it is often the best course for fast sales growth for inventors with high margin products, where the product's wholesale sales price is at least twice the product's manufacturing costs. This chapter covers how to find a strong marketing partner to sell your product.

There are several principles to follow when selecting a partner. The partner needs to be selling to the right market and they also need to be able to generate significant revenue per year with your concept. The partner should also have a strong reputation and have had strong sales growth. But the critical point is to work with companies where the inventor can find someone inside the company who is willing to push management to carry your product. Ideally this person is a regional manager or marketing person with enough clout to move the project forward. The marketing partner can be chosen from a wide range of businesses: a manufacturing company that makes other products it sells, a distributor who sells to the same target market, a manufacturer's representative firm that plays an important role in a particular market, a large end user of an industrial product, or even a major retailer looking to sign a private label agreement for its stores.

Potential Marketing Partners

Typically when people think of a marketing partner, they are thinking of bigger companies that have large marketing and sales staff. Those companies can be good partners, but they are also partners that can take a long time to sell. What you need from a marketing partner is a commitment to take the product for a period of time, which means a marketing partner is a very broad term for inventors. For example, a retailer is a partner if it agrees to buy a fixed number of units for three years in return for an additional ten percent discount and an exclusive sales agreement.

Companies with Branded Offerings

Products and services are branded when they are sold under a name the company promotes. The Geek Squad sells branded computer repair services and the Crank Brothers sell branded bike repair products to bike shops. Companies with branded products typically sell through established distribution channels, compete with many other companies, and have a somewhat steady stream of business. These companies will be interested in marketing inventor products when those deals improve their competitive situation.

Distributors

Distributors often look for exclusive deals on "hot" products or services that have strong customer demand since it boosts all of their products sales.

Retailers

They already buy lots of private label products, which are typically non-exclusive agreements for a product with the retailers name on it. A private label agreement is one option to an inventor when the retailer makes a three or four year commitment.

Companies that Market Others' Products

Many markets have one or two companies that market products from overseas manufacturers or small US companies. They also make strong marketing partners.

Finding Potential Partners

Finding partners starts with the target customer. Anyone who is active with your target customer is a potential partner. Make a list of all the companies and organizations that interact with your targeted customers. The best way to find these companies is by using directories that are posted on web sites for trade magazines and associations and from exhibitors lists from industry trade shows.

Trade magazines typically have directories where you can often get a list of manufacturers, manufactures' representatives and distributors. As an example, I learned rock salt lamps are popular in Pakistan, both for their soft ambient mood lighting and because the rock salt lamp releases ions when the light is on that have some medicinal value. To look into potential partners I did an internet search for lighting retailer trade magazines and at the top of the list was the site for Home Lighting and Accessories, the trade magazine for lighting retailers. The site contained a directory for manufacturers, manufacturing representatives, and some distributors. I also subscribed to the magazine (most trade magazines are available at no charge) so I could keep up with the industry. You can also find trade magazines in *Gale's Source of Publications and Broadcast Media*, which is available in larger libraries.

Associations can also be located using the internet in exactly the same way as trade magazines. For the associations related to lighting I found several sources but the best one was the National Home Furnishings Association. The association's directory for products contained a list of many manufacturers and distributors and a list of auxiliary members had the names of manufacturers' representatives. *Gale's Book of Associations,* also available at libraries, contains the most comprehensive list of associations that I've run across.

Trade shows are another good source for finding potential partners because most key market suppliers will exhibit at a trade show. Most shows have directories that list all the exhibitors, what their products are and contact information for each company. Your best bet is to just call the trade show sales office and ask for a copy of last year's show directory. You can find the right trade shows contacts in trade magazines and at www.tsnn.com, which is a comprehensive web site directory of both big and small trade shows.

When Marketers are Receptive to a Deal

Marketing partners take on product from an inventor when it helps enhance their overall market presence. Inventors should research the target marketer to understand what sales approach will work best. I've listed a variety of reasons that might make the marketing partner be receptive to your offer.

New Market Trends

Downloading music for fees, cell phone conference calls among teenagers, backyard water ponds, and hybrid golf clubs are all new trends where some companies are winners and others losers. For inventors, especially ones that are users of the product, these trends open up opportunities because companies participating in the market don't know for sure what the fast changing market wants, and may use an inventor's product to better explore the market. Scrapbooking is a good example: that market went from low sales to five billion dollars in sales in a just a few years. Many of the new products in that market came from inventors or others who were diehard scrapbookers--they knew what the market wanted because they were one of those target customers.

Product Line Gaps

Marketers can't afford a hole in their product line because companies avoid having multiple sources of supply, which is expensive and complicated. Having an incomplete product line causes companies to dump one marketer in favor of another marketer with a complete line to keep hassles and expenses down. Limited supply sources are even more important to service providers, since both companies and consumers tend to prefer just one supplier. A potential marketer will be receptive from a proposal from an inventor who fills in a product line. Filling a product gaps causes the marketer to get all of his products or services into more outlets, thereby increasing sales across the board.

Improved Margins

Distributors and retailers might sell a product at a 30 to 40% margin. If the distributor commits to a three year deal for an exclusive selling arrangement he might receive an additional five to seven percent margin, either as a discount or as a share of the profits. That's a good deal for distributor.

Increased Revenue

Certain functions are critical for a marketer to continue, such as newsletters, service support, or sponsorships of events, to keep connected to their customers. But often those activities barely break even in profitability for their companies, and the marketer is looking for ways to create new revenue streams to help cover all of their fixed marketing costs. Small companies, who have trouble creating enough revenue to afford an effective marketing program might add an inventor's product to build up their revenue stream to help offset these fixed marketing costs.

Change in Top Personnel

New management is always looking to make an impact on their employees and the market. They will go out of their way to look at new ideas and concepts from inventors/entrepreneurs in the hope that they might have an idea that will sell. This situation is especially advantageous for inventors because they can often get right to the top management people in the company.

Unable to Fund Their Own Introduction

Sometimes the best marketers to approach are mid- to small-size companies that lack the resources to introduce a product on its own. Look for companies in the market that feature mostly accessories or peripheral equipment or services for companies and can't afford a major introduction. With the work you've done developing your idea, and the other resources you bring with you, you and the marketer can succeed together.

Choosing the Best Marketing Partner

- Determine your investment required to manufacturer the product.

- Determine if the marketer is capable of delivering annual sales levels 15 to 20 times your investment, otherwise you won't be able to recoup your money.

- The project should represent a 10 to 25% increase in sales to the marketer. If the project is less than 10% it will be hard to generate excitement in the marketer as the project just won't have enough impact. A 10 to 25% increase will make a significant difference to both the company sales totals and bottom line.

- Potential targets have several of the characteristics that make marketers receptive to a deal.

Types of Deals for Marketers

Inventors' deals with manufacturers can be set up in a number of ways. I've listed an array of deal structures you can suggest to marketers to find the one that suits them best.

Firm Purchase Commitment

The simplest inventor deal is a two to three year purchase commitment that's large enough to help the inventor sell all the products it can afford to make. Retailers are a good example of a company that will do this, as well as distributors or integrators, who buy your product and then include it in as a component of their own product. An exhaust system manufacturer, for example, is an integrator who might buy large volumes of an innovative component from an inventor that it will incorporate into its final product.

Firm Purchase Agreements in Return for Considerations

The agreement might call for exclusive rights nationally or in a territory for either a short time or it could be for the duration of the agreement. Rather than a total exclusive agreement, the consideration might be that certain features or applications are exclusive to the marketing partner. For example a chain of skateboard shops might have exclusive rights to a new style of polyurethane wheels on a skateboard, but not exclusive rights to the entire skateboard line. Agreements also can be entered with price concessions in additional other considerations. In return for a firm long term agreement you might have to give up both, and might also need to offer protected pricing, which you can only raise under certain restricted circumstances.

Private Label Agreements

A private label agreement is really no different than the first two options, except that rather than branding your product or service with your name, it is instead branded with the marketer's company name. For example you might sell your skateboard wheels with the name of the distributor or retailer on the box. This is the deal that most often works if you are selling to a marketing company that sells products from overseas and other small manufacturers.

The deals you might suggest here can typically be handled by a purchase order or straight buy and sell agreement. Web sites with simple sample forms you can utilize for a buy sell or private label agreement are: *www.albusiness.com* (my top choice); *www.legalforms.com; www.findlegalforms.com; www.lawdepot.com; www.americalawyer.com* and *www.findlaw.com*.

The next chapter covers how to land an inside contact to make your sale easier.

Chapter 18

Landing an Inside Contact – the Easiest Way to Sell Your Product

Inventors will have a far easier time striking a deal with a marketer or distributor when they have a strong supporter inside the potential partner company. You want to find the supporter early before you make any formal sales calls. The contact can then help you fine tune your presentations to the company's needs. They will also advocate for your project inside the company, urging management to move ahead with your offer. Typically you want to find either a regional manager or a marketing manager to help you.

You don't need to go with your hat in your hand when working on an inside contact, they actually gain as much as you do when they present the project, in fact it is a win-win situation for them. If they bring the project to the company and the company successfully introduces the concept, the inside contact looks like a real go-getter that is helping the company advance. If the project doesn't go through, they still look like a go-getter, an image that will help them at some point in their career. The following steps will usually get you an inside contact with a potential partner company.

1. Show consumers want your product. You won't strike your best deal by just showing your invention. Instead, you want to show positive first market research with intriguing possibilities, and then tell partners that your concept seems so strong that you feel it will do best if you partner up with a marketer immediately to exploit the opportunity. That approach allows you to enlist partners in the beginning phases of an exciting opportunity, rather than, from their perception, after you failed to raise money to market your own company.

2. Start with a salesperson. You can meet salespeople by requesting literature and attending association meetings. You can also attend trade shows and meet sales people just by walking up and talking to them in their booth. Try to walk the shows early in the morning or late in the afternoon when the number of real customers is low. Once you meet salespeople ask to take them to lunch as you need some input from them on a concept you think might work in the market.

3. Use a product introduction to explain your concept and the research you've put into the project. Don't try to sell the salesperson, just show him or her the presentation with the observation that you're trying to decide what would be a good next step.

4. Ask for his or her input on your idea and what could be done to make the concept go. They might ask for more detailed information on the concept in which case you can ask them to sign a Statement of Confidentiality. Take the salesperson's comments in and be receptive to what he or she has to say. Then ask if this is a concept that his or her company might be interested in. More than likely the person will have quite a few comments on how it could be done with his or her company, with suggestions on making the concept "just right" for the target company.

5. Arrange to meet regional or marketing managers. If the salesperson is on board, make at least some of the changes he or she suggested and then ask the salesperson if he or she could set up a meeting with the regional manager or marketing manager. Usually they can meet with you, either when the manager comes to town, at a trade show, or you might be able to visit the company's location.

6. Use contact to help set up the presentation with the company. Once you convey your concept to the regional or marketing manager, they will be able to set up a key meeting with the right people at their company. Often they will introduce you

and give a little sales pitch about how your concept could have a significant impact on the company before you even get started.

Show Consumers Want Your Product

You should always start by showing that you have researched your product and that it has broad consumer appeal. You should start ideally by showing how you are a user of the product. You show other people want your product with observational research which shows why they want the product, and comparative product research which shows they prefer your product to others on the market.

Observational Research

One type of observational research consists of just watching end users use the product, noting each step the user takes and then asking the user why they do every step. This is the type of research that many consumer giants such as Procter and Gamble use regularly. If you observe four or five users in action you will notice that they experience, and compensate for, different drawbacks to products or services, drawbacks they may not even realize exists. If you ask people about how they are compensating, they will either affirm that is a problem, or explain it is not a problem. You want to be able to say that a high percentage of the people you observe have experienced the problem your product solves.

Comparative Research

This process simply asks buyers or end users to evaluate your product against three to seven other products and then asks them to rank the products or concepts both by value and by likelihood of buying. It is useful to do comparative research for both directly competing products or services that achieve the same purpose as yours and for other products or services of a similar type that a company or consumer might buy.

For example, with the Garlic Twist, a new more effective way to prepare garlic for cooking, you would buy every other product that also prepares garlic for cooking. Then, if the Garlic Twist cost $8.00, you would also obtain four or five other kitchen items, with a cost of $4.00 to $12.00. Make sure that some of the products are strong sellers, or your research won't matter much since no one wants any of the products you are comparing yours to. For effective comparative research, don't tell the participants what product is yours.

To start research, just find 10 to 20 people to review all the products. Ask them to rank the products on how likely they are to buy it, with "one" being the most likely to purchase. Also ask them to rank the products by value, with "one" being the most valuable product. You should be able to determine if people are likely to buy your product, and what is the price point they would buy it at. If people place your product's value by products that are $4.00, then that means its value is about

$4.00. Prepare a graph report on your findings to show potential contacts.

Finding Industry Salespeople

Every market and industry has sales people who are usually knowledgeable and very helpful. The best way to contact sales people is either to meet them at trade shows or trade associations or to simply request product information. When you read trade magazines, you'll notice that they have extensive new product sections, or in the case of service businesses, new services that companies want to promote or sell. Request information for any product or service that is listed in the new product/service section. You are not necessarily interested in the information about the product or service but in the name of the company contact that will typically come on a letter that will arrive with the literature. You can then call up that contact and ask questions such as how their product or service is sold, who are the most important companies in the market, what are the new market trends, and which companies have had the most successful new introductions. You might also ask a contact that is especially helpful if you can contact him or her again in the future.

Other Potential Helpers - Trade Associations and Chambers of Commerce

Many industries or markets have trade associations which are groups of people, including retailers, distributors, marketers, and purchasing agents. Trade associations work for the betterment of companies in the industry. They have volunteer committees of members who do most of the work of the association. You can learn about an industry by joining an association and volunteering to be on committees. Marketing committees can be especially helpful for a new entrepreneur since they typically have volunteers that are in marketing for their own companies. You can find trade associations in Gale's Book of Associations, which can be found at most large libraries.

Local Chambers of Commerce have monthly meetings and you should try attending at least one meeting in your town as there may be contacts that can help you. Chambers of Commerce frequently have people who like to help new businesses and some Chambers have active mentoring programs that can give you a sounding board for your project.

About the Authors

Edith G. Tolchin

Edith G. Tolchin, "The Sourcing Lady" (SM), "invented" **EGT Global Trading** in 1997, with a goal to link U.S. inventors with Asian manufacturers, to provide a "one-stop import service" for sourcing, quality control, manufacturing, production testing, international financing, air/ocean shipping, customs clearance arrangements, and dock-to-door delivery. Edie began her career in import and international trade in the 1970s, fresh out of New York University, with a New York City importer of frozen fish and bicycles. She has worked with both large and small importers, handling commodities from salted nuts to chemicals and waxes, to wearing apparel and toys. Ms. Tolchin holds a U.S. Customs Broker License, and has extensive experience with Customs and Border Protection, and customs brokers in various products and issues, including binding rulings, duty protests and drawbacks. She is a product safety expert, and is a

Professional Member of the United Inventors Association.

Aside from travel, one of Ms. Tolchin's favorite hobbies is freelance writing for many publications. She particularly enjoys contributing articles to Inventors Digest magazine (www.inventorsdigest.com).

EGT Global Trading specializes in offshore manufacturing services for inventions of textiles and sewn-items, bags, baby and fashion accessories, unique arts & crafts items, and household inventions. Edie Tolchin regularly provides presentations for inventors' organizations and trade shows throughout the USA on topics such as "Importing Basics for Inventors" "Consumer Product Safety Improvement Act – Product Safety," and "Offshore Manufacturing for Inventors."

For free brochure and lit packet, please contact: *EGT Global Trading*, P.O. Box 231, Florida, NY 10921 USA. Phone (845) 321-2362, e-mail: EGT@warwick.net, webpage: www.egtglobaltrading.com

Don Debelak

Don Debelak has been working with new products and inventions for over 25 years and is the author of four of the best-known invention books of the last 15 years. He also was the author or Entrepreneur Magazine's Bright Idea column on inventions for over seven years. Don has spent his career marketing products for new and small businesses, writing numerous business plans for raising money, both from investors and banks. Don has worked with all types of business, especially as a

consultant for the University of St. Thomas Small Business Center, from small one man service business to high-tech ventures that are set up to raise money and launch a new product.

The One Stop Invention Shop, onestopinventionshop.net, is an inventor assistance site run by Don Debelak and a group of expert associates, including Edith Tolchin, the manufacturing and outsourcing associate. The site is dedicated to help inventors with every step of the invention process, from product development to manufacturing and marketing their products.

Some services include product introduction plans, marketing and business plans as well as one-on-one consulting. Don also provides market penetration assistance for international inventors by preparing action plans and sales and marketing assistance.

Don also runs a Catalog Marketing Program at selltocatalogs.com. This program helps inventors and new product entrepreneurs launch their product sales in catalogs, allowing them to prove their products' potential to help them launch their products in other markets.

Eric Debelak

Eric Debelak has been working with Don Debelak since 2004. He is the Editor of the popular One Stop Invention Shop Newsletter, a free bi-monthly newsletter with lots of free help for inventors, and has been the driving force behind  the Don Debelak's Catalog Marketing Program, selltocatalogs.com, that has sold over $500,000 of products in its first two years.